NORTH AND NORTH AGAIN

I dedicate this book to Gina, who knew the bad times – and they were many.

NORTH AND NORTH AGAIN

by
D. BRIAN PLUMMER

HUDDLESFORD PUBLICATIONS

The line drawings throughout this book are the work of Martin Knowelden, and anyone wishing to contact him regarding his work can do so through the publishers.

Huddlesford Publications
Hawthorn House
Bowdell Lane
Brookland
Kent TN29 9RW

First Published 1987

ISBN 0 907827 06 3

Set by D. P. Media Ltd, Hitchin, Hertfordshire
Printed and bound by Biddles Ltd, Guildford and King's Lynn

Contents

FATHOM AND FRIEND

—1—

Life Certainly Doesn't Begin at Forty

I'M NOT QUITE sure who it was that said 'Life begins at forty', though I have the oddest feeling that such a saying must be attributed to Groucho Marx, Mel Brookes, or maybe someone else who considers it witty to concoct a very unfunny and very untrue epigram which gives those approaching that magic age, at least a hope there are better things to come. In fact nothing could be further from the truth, for when a person reaches the age of forty, it appears as though that Great Mechanic in the Sky decides that this particular model of homo sapien is not only ready for a full service, but is of a suitable age for a very testing MOT. By this age several of the parts of the said vehicle are wearing badly and in some cases failing to function.

In fact, as soon as a man tops double-twenty an odd variety of physical and mental malaises seem to literally bombard him, ailments ranging from nervous breakdowns to ulcers, even though just prior to the victim reaching the 'magic age' he may resemble a very sound viable hybrid twixt the winner of The Krypton Factor and the fictional super hero Doc Savage. However, on one's fortieth birthday, for some reason or other, the whole works suddenly seem to go a shade awry and one finds forty-year-old friends, who have never been ill in their lives opening birthday cards and complaining about back ache, hiatus hernias and all manner of ills which don't seem to trouble Krypton winners, or the 'men of bronze types'. True, no one of that age ever complains about diseases such as piles, but who in the world is going to admit to being afflicted with piles, anyway. (It's curious, but I've never been able to spell haemoroids.)

Some of my close associates reach the age of forty and promptly up-sticks and die of coronaries or allied complaints even though they have just, in their thirty-ninth year that is, been nominated as local squash champion of the year – not that I know many squash players mind you, but it goes to show the lie of 'Life begins at forty', for in many cases squash racket in hand, life for some has ended at the said date. However, I was blissfully aware that that couldn't happen to me for besides the fact that I've never been inside a squash court I didn't consider myself what Reader's Digest class as 'the coronary type'. True, I'm a born hypochondriac – a quality I've inherited from Mam who started dying at the age of nineteen and finished the task quite successfully at the age of eighty-five – and I have to force myself never to open the pages of *Black's Medical Dictionary* lest I should be instantly smitten by a lethal attack of Vietnamese Bladder or something similarly exotic and equally unlikely. However, as I approached my fortieth birthday I put all thoughts of illness out of my head, even though I did mull over the sobering fact that I was approaching the last furlong of the three-score-years-and-ten racecourse called life.

The age of forty is, I suppose, not meant to spring out on a man like a mugger out of the shadows – one day he's thirty-nine, hale and hearty, and that night some vampire squats on his chest, sucking the life virtue, energy and vitality, leaving him to open his birthday cards like a sear and yellow leaf, but I'm afraid in my case it was so. The eve of my approaching birthday I spent with two associates I'd known for some time, not even breathing a word of the oncoming fateful birthday. Come to think of it, I didn't feel old, though I confess the glances I cast at the mini-skirted dolly birds bubbling past with their glasses of Babycham were more a result of habit rather than lust. We sat on the outskirts of what is today referred to as a 'hen party', a group of ladies who were normally respectable women who at the time in question were temporarily behaving like a bunch of extras from a Mad Max film and centring around a rather jaded and tired-looking 'bride to be' who, frankly, looked as though everyone, but everyone, had seen better days. Deirdre had been married before – many times and oft, if the snippets of conversation we overheard were true and had probably been up and down the aisle so often she was suffering from forced-march fatigue rather than prenuptual nerves.

'Better luck next time', toasted one hideous witch whose plunging neckline revealed only a plunging neck, and upon this statement the whole band burst into hysterics coming out with marriage jokes, loss of virginity and a host of other incongruous and inappropriate quips about the future of the clearly much-used and much-experienced Deirdre.

Deirdre – God, do people still call their children Deirdre – it's a hell of a punishment if they do – joined in the pre-marital revelry, her face creasing with laughter, revealing a set of aluminium-type fillings of the kind sported by a James Bond villain who is quite capable of biting through a Chubb lock to despatch Roger Moore. I had the oddest feeling that only a really desperately lonely sheet metal worker from Coventry could find the amalgam-mouthed Deirdre attractive. Deirdre, so the banter led us to believe, was starting out on her fourth marriage and thus the jokes about violated chastity and pre-marital advice shouted by the rest of the group seemed as futile as insisting Evil Knieval wear an L-plate.

Next to me sat Abe Sapersteen, a Birmingham fish wholesaler, whose acidic tongue could etch its way through a bank vault, and who gave me an odd feeling of verbal inadequacy whenever I was in his company.

'Ach, look at that crowd of harridans,' he hissed, and added a rider which would have drawn a wince from a mule skinner let alone a rabbi. 'The last time I saw such a collection was around a cauldron. Jesus, what a bunch of witches.'

There's something about fish that brings out the eloquent savant in a person and of this I'm sure. Every fish wholesaler I know has a tongue like a whip and I'm half-convinced that Jesus only went to the sea of Galilee to get disciples because he knew that the quick-tongued sort of bloke wouldn't be too far from the wholesale fish market. During wartime years Mam used to force-feed me ration book herring, ramming them down my throat, trying to convince me that the herring and other aquatic inedibles were brain food. I pointed out that Specky Jenkins, our village idiot, was a fishmonger's son and the herrings hadn't helped him much, but she continued to push fish down my throat, fork touching my epiglottis to make sure I swallowed them despite my protests and logic. The torture ceased when she read that fish could in addition to producing Einsteins also produce eczema and Mam, being the world's greatest hypochondriac, promptly developed a nasty rash at the mere mention of a herring, so she stopped cramming me with fish.

Sapersteen brought me back from the realms of hypochondriac mothers, fish-eating village idiots and my childhood ration book world with a sharp reminder of my own age.

'Look at the witches,' he was muttering. 'Hideous – the youngest must be at least forty!'

I glanced at my watch noticing that the witching hour of the magic age was a mere hour and a half away, so I bade farewell to the fish-selling savant who kept sneering at the group of temptresses, and left the pub to the unlady-like refrains of the menopausal songsters singing a song about a lady of Jerusalem who was certainly no racist as she did amazing and uncaring things to Jew, Arab and Christian alike. I turned the key in my lock noting the time as 12.30 am and as the icy cold of my bleak and empty cottage hit me, I muttered a quick, 'Happy birthday, Bri', and limped geriatrically to bed.

Saturday, and I lay in bed until 8 am wondering what the future held in store for a guy who had made it half-way to becoming an octogenarian, listening, a smile on my face, to our postman who was clearly not a plant-lover muttering, 'Bastard!' as he climbed through the mesh of unkempt roses which covered my porch entrance. He left giving the door a deft kick, licking the blood from his lacerated and torn hands, after having dropped one card in my porch – a grubby second-hand birthday card, the first recipient of which had been called Robin and aged eight, sent by Rosie my class register monitor who had argued logically, I suppose, that because I knew her date of birth it was reasonable that she should know mine. I showed her my driving licence and she uttered a shrill whistle of amazement, literally agog, that anyone could have been born so long ago and still be around to talk about it. To kids of Rosie's age and background, anyone over twenty-five is senile. A week ago she had said, giving her nose an unladylike brush with her sleeve, 'I ain't getting married young like my sister did – a right cock-up that.' (Rosie has a way with words although considering her sister's reasons for matrimony perhaps it was an apt turn of phrase.) 'I'm waiting till I'm eighteen. I wanna see a bit of life first.' Funnily enough I saw Rosie yesterday. She's twenty-two, has three kids and has had all her teeth taken out – there's a moral there if only I can find it! I brushed aside the theory she had been raped repeatedly by an unfrocked dentist, smiled and passed her by.

To return, I bent down to pick up the card and felt an agonising pain in my back, a sharp flashing spurt of agony as though someone had dealt me a God Almighty blow across my lumbar region, or I had been charged by a bull who hadn't even had the decency to be goaded by a quick 'Torro'. I tried to slither up my porch, clutching my rotting window frames (mine is not a pleasant house), wincing and groaning and wondering what the heck had happened to me. Yet afternoon still found me bent-double, knuckles to the floor like one of the 'almost' men Leaky keeps searching for in the Olduvai Gorge of Africa. Knuckles to the floor I ambled from room to room still musing over Rosie's second-hand card and the fact that she considered me so old that my knowledge of Roman history had been gleaned first-hand. At that moment in time I felt as though Rosie could be right.

I gave in on Monday and phoned the doctor's. I hate surgeries, doctors, hospitals *etc*, though my mother delighted in associating with such people in such places and would have gladly worked in an intensive care unit, free of charge, if only to be near to people who may have understood her myriad complaints. Hell, it's not just Mam who is hospital crazy. Most of afternoon TV viewing consists of programmes about Australian hospitals which are so gooey and love-orientated that it makes one wonder what the hell is going on if there's a pause between 'Scalpel' and 'Forceps'. Boy oh boy, would I refuse an operation 'Down Under' if these programmes are anything to go by.

Fortunately my own doc is a genius and I'm so confident in him that I limp in to his surgery in agony only to breeze out minutes later feeling great, which could prove one of two things, that either he has Messianic healing powers or I'm a bigger hypochondriac than my mother. This time not so, however. He bent me double – not exactly difficult as I was just about there anyway, put his knee in my back, jerked hard (I promised to tell him everything I know about anyone), pronounced I had a slipped disc, and booked me into hospital, pronto. Piltdown-fashion I put on my trousers while he studied my medical card and uttered a cryptic if hurtful, 'A slipped disc is one of the most common problems which besets the over forties' thereby, I might add, touching a nerve more painful than the one I had displaced in my back.

I can honestly boast I behave like a real he-man when I am in hospital. I shout, scream at the slightest touch and wallow in self-pity. I also find it very offensive if a nurse so much as mentions if I have had the use of some of my bodily functions on a particular day and steadfastly refrain to answer. However, it is easy to feel sorry for oneself when one is lying in bed with feet at forty-five degrees balanced by we-have-ways-of-making-you-talk weights. However, what is horrendous is that for three weeks I was strapped up in this position with nothing to do except read and it would take a bloody contortionist to understand anything more intellectual than the *Beano* with one's legs hanging in this position. What made it even worse was the loon in the bed opposite who played the Vic Damone tape, 'Outside of Space I Hang Suspended', over and over and over again without even realising it was causing offence.

However, to break the awful monotony of hospital life and to relax the muscles of one's spine, the hospital authorities prescribe a drug called Diazapam, and just as homocide, genocide, and manslaughter is technical jargon for good old-fashioned murder, so Diazapam is just another word for good old-fashioned Valium, the drug prescribed by the bucketful if the daily papers are correct, to bored, listless, middle class housewives who are disenchanted with life but not so disenchanted as to go out and seek employment of some sort. The drug, so I am assured, allows such ladies to be soothed, calmed, acting as a gentle palliative, allowing them to trip happily out of their tipsy trances just in time to greet Rover-driving husbands with a dry Martini, and revive just long enough to trip out for a spot of wife swopping. Hell, I really must go out and get a better-paid job, these Roche chemically propelled people seem to get all the fun.

Anyway, that's the way the drug is supposed to work – on norms that is. On people like me things just don't pan out as expected. Far from a soothing palliative bringing peace, tranquillity and muscle relaxation, the drug sends me raving mad, stark-staring bonkers, more out of my mind that I normally am in fact.

Now when roused to anger I have a reputation, maybe just maybe unjust, of having a rather sharp, spiteful tongue – not witty or clever and certainly not courageous, just a bit on the spiteful side, but such a septic tongue is kept in place by the fact that I am by nature a coward and am well aware of the physical repercussions which could follow an outburst of what I might consider to be eloquence. So out of crass cowardice I remain totally schtum even when I have a gem on the end of my tongue waiting to be said. Valium, no that makes me sound like a bored housewife – Diazapam lets me slip off my cloak of cowardice and lets the real Mr Hyde me escape. The trouble is under this slightly mad exterior there is obviously an even madder interior, and thus my eloquent outbursts usually degenerate to barmy comments, meaningless babble and insane and stupid insults. (It's the Diazapam, Doc – I'm as sane as the next without it.) However, once on the drug it would be harder to find a more stupid, big-mouthed lout than myself, and that is putting it mildly and in no time flat I had won the most unpopular person in the hospital award by a clear fifteen-round decision. Examples to follow.

Diazapam takes a short time to take effect on me, but on the second day of the administration of the drug the slightly reclusive Dr Jeckyl gave rise to the raving barmy Mr Hyde. That morning an elegant, highly articulate, turbanned Sikh surgeon strolled down the ward accompanied by a retinue of very servile nurses and twittering, adoring students. He paused at my bedside noting my angular if recumbent position, and nodded his elegant turbanned head in approval.

' 'Ope your head gets better soon, mate,' I quipped. (My God, I'm no racist – I have Sikh friends galore and twelve Sikh Godchildren.)

He said nothing but his sneer indicated that the English Raj in India must have been an awful mistake and that perhaps the Black Hole of Calcutta was an excellent residence for folk of my calibre. He left contemptuously and dignified as only a Sikh can be, while I went into hysterics about the Biblical quote, 'Physician heal thyself'.

Across the ward a victim of terminal cancer had perhaps unwisely and certainly perhaps a little belatedly bought a copy of *Playboy* or a similar periodical which has very little story line, but perhaps doesn't really need one. A visiting cleric, po-faced and almost certainly uninvited, by the way the cancer victim was trying to stow his magazine under his mattress, was in attendance. A photograph of a large and rounded backside of one of the couldn't-care-less ladies of the magazine was protruding from under the mattress and the vicar was eyeing the vision with a hint of amazement on his rather vacant face while trying to offer condolences to the *Playboy*-reading geriatric who was probably hoping the 'Here After' was also the abode of Hugh Heffner type birds.

'Cheer up old chap, it could be worse,' the man of God uttered, rather stupidly I thought.

'How could it, you stupid sod? The poor bastard is dying,' I exploded, my emotional outburst brought about, I confess, more by Diazapam than by sympathy.

'You callous sod,' shouted the ingrowing toenail, and turned up Vic Damone, still hanging suspended, even louder, full blast in fact.

Nurse Moore, a calm diplomat to the last, rushed over and hurriedly cleaned my face.

'Just giving a wash before visiting time,' she muttered, pushing the flannel deep inside my mouth, down as far as my oesophagus to stifle the cries, blasphemies and abuse I was hurling at the embarrassed cleric, trying to soothe the *Playboy*-coveting, ticket-booking traveller to 'the land from which no one' – well, you know the rest, and worst of all at the ingrowing toenail and his silly sod song.

Mr Hardy, another terminal cancer case, and a very decent chap whose loss will be one this spiteful world will surely miss, tried to break the stony and hostile silence. (Nurse Moore still had sponge rammed into my trachea.)

'There's a case of haemorrhoids coming in tomorrow,' he said, almost apologetically – and I can see why.

Sponge removed, the Diazapam-induced Dr Hyde took over immediately.

'Make a change from that bloody Lucozade.' I roared with laughter at my own inanity while Nurse Moore, seeing the gaping opening and being a born opportunist went half-way into my lungs with the sponge to stifle the abuse.

'If Mr Hardy dies in the night, can I have his 'jamas? There's a hole in mine,' I managed to splutter.

'Yes of course you can, my boy,' said Mr Hardy cheerfully, and even under the influence of the dreaded Diazapam, I felt a real rat about the incident.

'Bet you don't get invited to cocktail parties,' shouted Ingrowing Toenail.

'That's 'cos I don't know many cock tales,' I hooted back derisively.

The vicar, with the dying *Playboy* enthusiast, winced visibly and left, slinking out like an embarrassed wombat. Nurse Prickett came on after Nurse Moore and the less said about that the better. Sufficient to say she left in tears after an hour, and my relationship with Ingrowing Toenail worsened slightly to the point of him uttering threats against my life. Poor old Mr Hardy, on his last legs, tried to pour oil on troubled waters but as these waters were from a bottle of some sort that Ingrowing Toenail had produced like a magician from beneath the bed sheets, and hurled across the room at me, perhaps disinfectant rather than oil would have been a more suitable additive.

Diazapam is a cruel drug. The party drunk who has been a pain in the neck all night annoying all and sundry, remembers nothing of his misdemeanours the morning after, or perhaps only vaguely recalls the various incidents of the night before. The Diazapam drunk, once the drug has been withdrawn, remembers all too painfully the havoc he has caused and as the last remnant of the drug seeped from my body via various unmentionable processes, the month I had endured, the misery I had caused, began to strike me like sheet lightning, particularly as Nurse Prickett passed the bed, nose in air, eyes straight ahead.

They allowed the Ingrowing Toenail to be discharged an hour earlier than me, thereby giving him a head start, so to speak, for relationships were a little strained to say the very least, and he passed my bed muttering, 'Nutter', and bobbing his tongue out in a manner not really befitting a thirty-seven-year-old. I said goodbye to every nurse, who curiously enough seemed too preoccupied with bed-making to reply to my farewells.

'I trust you see my head is still unwell,' sneered the Sikh specialist, before darting into the gent's toilet.

Only, and I mean only, Nurse Moore greeted me cordially and seemed almost sorry to see me go.

'I've seen many people, normal people,' she eyed me as if wishing for a second opinion, 'react strangely when given Diazapam.'

'Look,' I said, somewhat sheepishly, 'I'll buy you a present or at least get you one,' I countered, as I realised I was on my uppers at the time. 'Do you eat rabbit?' I asked.

'I couldn't look at one since that horrible disease (myxamatosis) has struck them down,' she said, wrinkling her nose.

'Give some of the virus to 'im,' shouted the Ingrowing Toenail who must have had car trouble and was just starting-up and passing us.

'Yeh, the first symptoms are ingrowing toenails, mate,' I countered. But the irony was obviously lost as he wound up the window of his car, bobbed a quick tongue, mimed something unspeakable with his forearm, and drove off.

I immediately struck Ingrowing Toenail off my list of friends and returned to the patient and saintly Nurse Moore.

'Duck is the only meat eaten by our entire family,' she mused carefully, and my heart sank.

Lichfield and its surrounding fields is so heavily shot-over that the flicker of a mallard green bird invites a hail of lead such as greeted famous last words like, 'Over the top, men'. In fact anyone who eats a Lichfield-shot mallard stands a chance of going down with 'lead poison' shakes. However, us Plummers are ever inventive, a shade dirty, untidy and even dishonest, but nevertheless inventive, and I had a plan hatching. I hitched a lift home with Emrys Powell, a dustbin collector supposedly happily married (whatever that means), but who picks up an amazing collection of jaded off-centre lovelies at the local singles club simply by telling them he's an archaeologist – fine providing no one asked him to spell his occupation which would really throw him. Still, no one's perfect – as I've said, I've never been able to spell haemoroids though I admit it's not a subject about which I'd freely talk at a singles club in an endeavour to pick up wayward birds.

Collar up, I walked to where Emrys had parked his dustbin wagon and found him sifting through some black plastic bag no doubt searching for a few Viking artifacts which were bound to pull a few hideous ladies at that night's singles club. Lichfield seems to be choc-a-bloc full of Dr Johnson signs, every corner or signpost seemed to mention the first British lexicographer though if the graffiti in the library toilets is anything to go by, there's a damned sight more than dictionary writing on the mind of the average Lichfieldian, and when the blinds are drawn and lights out the joint must really jump. I always pop in to the toilets to peruse a few snippets that Nigel Rees would have travelled a hundred miles to read, snippets which would cause Bronowski to subtitle *The Ascent of Man* as 'Was Your Journey Really Necessary', I must add. On the day in question, mind a boggle and spinal disc a tingle, I popped in to read the latest Lichfield news of the sort that doesn't make the front page of the *Lichfield Mercury*. A raging pervert, lonely or perhaps merely out to impress, had written, 'I am 10 inches long and 2 inches thick; anyone interested?', under which someone had written – 'Fascinated – how long is your "dick"?'. Still, it takes all sorts I suppose and it wouldn't do if everyone was just interested in ferrets and similar things or even archaeology for that matter.

Reading over, I turned back towards the cathedral pool. Lichfield has a cathedral so I've been told, I've never been there. The damned place always seems full of Americans, quoting Revelations, buying postcards of Britain's dullest city and chewing Wrigley's Spearmints – funny lot the Americans, I've always found. I turned past the cathedral pool where a host of old-age pensioners were literally queueing up to hurl bread crumbs at the water fowl which snootily select only the choicest morsels, allowing the rest to sink into the murky depths of the pool. I have it on good authority that there is a layer a good four inches thick of Tom Allison's 'Nowt taken out' fermenting on the bottom of the pool and Porky Arrowsmith says there's a five-hundred foot carp feeding off the waste bread crumbs down there. I don't believe him – he's prone to exaggeration – though he was dead right about last month's bus strike, I must admit. Anyway, back to the pool. Frankly, aside from feeding the water fowl, there's not a lot to do in Lichfield for the young or the old or for anyone for that matter. People seem to come there to die (usually at the age of 24) and apart from the occasional council-sponsored trip to watch the traffic lights change colour at Kennings Corner, there's only those bloody water fowl to keep the place buzzing. Indeed, so thickly are the old-age pensioners gathered around these water fowl that I believe that on long-service retirement a Lichfieldian receives a sack of bread crumbs or mill sweepings rather than a gold watch. However, it was the ducks rather than the bread crumbs that fascinated me, and, reader, if you can't guess the ending you too must also find it difficult to spell archaeologist or haemorrhoids.

A brief insight into my scatty off-the-beaten-track lifestyle now. I own and breed a type of mongrel greyhound called a lurcher, a none too subtle blend of collie/greyhound spiked with a dash of something else; thieving, poaching sorts of dogs not really the ideal pet for Mr Normal with 2.4 kids, wife and a mortgage, though a lot of these people seem to own them. Most lurchers if given half a chance, are rapacious hunters and mine are to the last, villainous chicken thieves who will even snatch up half-grown turkey poults and head for home to stock the 1½ acres of nettles and slabs I lyingly call a garden to friends with a variety of strange poultry, a little damaged perhaps, both in pride and body but invariably alive. Hence, after a really bad month my garden tends to look a little like Dorsington Manor Rare Breeds Poultry Trust in an off-season. Ordinarily I suppress this acquisitive tendency in my lurchers and once and only once did I encourage it.

I arose just as dawn was breaking that October morning and clanked down to town in my rusty old Ford van bought cheaply and maintained willingly but rather despairingly by the RAC who had been called out so many times to non-starts that there was no need to explain where my cottage was and I became on first-name terms with the RAC telephone operator who sympathised and wrote down my membership number from memory. So with my lurcher Fathom in the back of the van and an enticing bag of Mother's Pride crumbs in the front, we clanked, clanged and spluttered our way to the cathedral pool where the first light illuminated not only the multicoloured collection of mallard mongrels and call ducks but also a rather ragged old lady, bag of crumbs in hand trying to feed the brutes as daylight broke. Now frankly, I consider that anyone who gets up at daylight just to throw crumbs into a pond is little short of nuts, though considering the deed I was about to perpetrate, my own sanity certainly must be held in question. The old lady, bag of mixed morsels ranging from Mother's Pride crumbs to scraps of what I sincerely hope wasn't Christmas cake (it was October), was enticing a very off-hand snooty batch of wild fowl by a scatter of crumbs and a rather throaty 'Percy, come on Percy', and eventually her persistence or her 'Percy' (God, that sounds rude) paid off, for a mix of mallard and Judas call ducks waddled up the bank to take the first of the morning's offerings until they were nearly at the feet of the old lady clutching her bag of crumbs.

I edged nearer, my footsteps muffled by the morning mist and shouts of 'Percy'. Fathom yawned, pretending to be indifferent to the dastardly deed about to be perpetrated while all the time the ill-named wild fowl putted aimlessly around the old lady's feet, snapping up crumbs more out of boredom than hunger, I thought at the time. I slackened the slip and Fathom struck like lightning, grabbing the nearest white call duck bringing it to hand in an instant. I thrust the struggling, quacking bird into my Tesco bag and glanced up. I shall never forget that scene if I live to be a hundred. A look of blank disbelief passed over the old girl's face, a hybrid look of amazement and absolute horror as she glanced around wondering if the Game for a Laugh team were in the bushes chortling to themselves. For a moment I expected hysteria, screaming and howling like a banshee, but to my astonishment she simply returned to feeding the ducks who seemed totally unperturbed by the fate of their Tesco-bag-incarcerated colleague, though she continued to glance out of the corner of her eye to either await my next move or to welcome Matthew Kelly as he leaped out of the bushes, microphone in hand and inane look on face. I released Fathom's lead once more and another duck flashed into the bag. The old lady quietly put down her bag of crumbs still wondering if what she saw was a nightmare or just a practical joke being televised, and said sincerely, as if cautioning a small boy,

'I don't think you should be doing that, should you?'

As I have mentioned times before we Plummers are an inventive family even though we seem to be devoid of any other worthwhile attributes and quick as a flash I produced my RAC card.

'RAC, Royal Aquatic Club, madam. We have to remove a few of these water fowls to prevent overcrowding. We are restocking another pond with them' I said, using my very best authoritarian voice (I'd copied it from our local dustmen who refused to 'collect' if the black plastic bag has a rip).

'The white one looks dead,' said the old lady suspiciously, gazing into the bag. The poor devil had up and snuffed it out of sheer terror.

'No, you are mistaken,' I said, poking its bill. 'It is simply tranquilised.'

'Looks dead to me,' she repeated, even more suspiciously and I felt like Palin and Cleese doing the dead parrot sketch.

'You are not an expert on water fowl, madam,' I said, 'whereas' – a quick flash of RAC card again – 'I am.'

'Sorry,' she muttered, 'ever so sorry', while I silently thanked God I'd joined the RAC and not the AA, whose initials would have been a bit more difficult to corrupt.

'Oh,' she uttered and cajolingly said, 'Could you leave Percy like (the one who had not snuffed it), he's a favourite like.'

Pity fought a ding-dong battle with avarice in my criminal mind and came up a points winner. I released Fathom again and snatched up another white call duck, letting Percy flutter free.

'I could be in serious trouble for breaking my rules, madam,' I said sternly. 'I hope you will forget that I have released your pet.'

I felt a real rat. She reached into her purse and offered me a pound, but not even I sink that low – well, not all that often anway. I waved her offering aside.

'Simply forget it,' I said, and hot-footed it to the van with the old lady shouting,

'Thank you mister. God bless you mister. Thank you', as I clanged back to the cottage.

I despatched the other call duck (killed sounds awful particularly in the light of what the reader has just read), feathered and gutted them, noting how small the carcasses were and wondering if there can be all that much nourishment in Mother's Pride and currant buns and if I should chance my arm with another sortie to the pond. Discretion prevailed and I decided against another foray and clanged to the hospital where I intended to present Nurse Moore with the Tesco bag containing two plucked and dressed ducks. They left the 'swag' in a refrigerator as Nurse Moore was on leave for two weeks and I raced back to the van where two traffic wardens were examining it, wondering how in hell it had passed its MOT, let alone why it had no parking sticker.

'RAC collection,' I spluttered, flashing the go anywhere, do anything card and drove off leaving them wondering what in hell was going on.

A sick thought hit me about those ducks and their shelf companions in that deep freeze/refrigerator. What in hell does one keep in a hospital deep freeze? Were my two cadavers bundled next to a long-dead heart or an eagerly awaited kidney for a dialysis victim and I had an odd vision of a drunken surgeon sewing in a call duck to a renal vein. Worse still a vision of a Fleur de Lys pie packed twixt sundry piles of viscera flashed into my mind, but I blotted out all such thoughts knowing full well I could easily fill the next intake at the 'funny farm' if I let such notions develop.

I met Nurse Moore a month later in the MEB shop in fact, when I was making a heart-felt plea to the manager to reconnect me as I had a sick mother. I did actually – she lived in South Wales!

'Thank you for the duck or should I say ducks. I really didn't expect them you know, but they were delicious. I invited over the cathedral choir for sandwiches and they did so enjoy them,' said Nurse Moore.

Something about 'Render unto Caesar that which is Caesar's' flashed into my mind but the embryonic quote refused to develop. I pulled the collar of my coat up and trudged back through the sleety rain to the van. Along the edge of the pool, macintosh and wellies, the old lady was hurling crusts of bread to the feeding ducks shouting, 'Percy, come on Percy', to a totally different breed of water fowl. I shook my head at the nature of human frailty and the inhumanity of the Midland Electricity Board and trudged home to my darkened electricity-free hovel. It was my first spell in hospital. I wish to God it had been my last, but that, as Kipling says, is another tale.

ODD ONE OUT

—2—

My Chosen Career?

'WAR IS HELL', said some American general, I'm not quite sure who and I'm too damned idle to look it up, but teaching in the average modern comprehensive school can't be rated too many points behind war in the jobs-I-wouldn't-like-to-do stakes. At the time of writing, people are bombarding the papers with attacks on a meek and mild children's programme called 'Grange Hill', a soap opera about a school which is far too tidy, totally lacking in mispelt graffiti and the kids too well behaved to be anything more than two paces away from RADA. Yet parents are writing in to complain that the programme has a corrupting effect on school children. Come off it Mums and Dads, things are a bloody sight worse than Grange Hill to the power of ten. I've worked in schools where the girls' 'lavs' were festooned with filth which would have brought a blush to the face of a hardened vice squad officer, and seen protection rackets set up and enforced in such a manner as to make Mario Puzo reach for his typewriter and dash off 'The Godfather 8, 9 and 10'. Teachers, most teachers, get a hell of a bad time in such schools, and matters are getting worse by the day. Thus, Mums and Dads who think Grange Hill is bad should stop writing to the BBC and go and see what the real live world of what is spuriously termed 'education' is all about.

How the hell I finished up in teaching I'll never know, or why I did would be more to the point, for from the time Mam – a surprisingly strong old lady despite the fact that her illnesses, real and imaginary, made her a Guinness Book of Records contender, illness stakes section – dragged me up Ffaldau Hill to the infants' school, slammed the door and left me to the hostile world of pig-tailed girls, sneering teddy bears and a rocking horse that sported teeth like a giant over-eager piranha, I've hated school. Come to think of it my fear of horses, called equaphobia by the more select, probably started in that infants' school reception group, for judging by the size of its incisors, that horse could have bitten off Muhamhad Ali's leg in a trice. I ran home at break-time and most other days afterwards until having lost all of the best of three falls to Mam at the school gates each day, I finally gave into the fact that I was stuck with being a victim of the 1870 Compulsory Education Act – a vicious bill which didn't pan out all that well by the way that things have turned out. By the time I was sixteen I put up only a slight struggle as Mam dragged me to the gates of the local grammar school.

I should never have taken up teaching as a career. I'm just not suited for the job. Maybe I would have made a good doctor, lawyer, or even a carpet fitter, but perhaps I'm just kidding myself, leastways about the doctor and lawyer bit. The chances are I'm not really cut out for any job, and it's a miracle that I've not joined Dad as leader of the jobless years ago, but somehow day by day, week by week, year by year, I've stuck the bloody job, even turning up on time some mornings. I'm not really suited to life amongst human beings, I just don't get on well with people, hate machinery, and I'd have joined the Armish years ago except for the fact that they preach cleanliness is next to Godliness and donate a great deal of money to their own church – and anyway they're 'into horses' in a big way and I've explained my feelings about those.

Somehow, someway, I just don't fit into the teaching profession – though I suppose I have to admit that in the last few years, I haven't really tried. Ironically I get on with the kids really well. In the district where I teach I have some twenty-odd Godchildren all called David Brian, supposedly in my honour – a somewhat questionable honour as four of them are in court on burglary charges in the next few weeks and one other for a shade worse. With kids I get on fine, but I just can't make a relationship with teachers in general and headmasters in particular. At each and every school I work the same pattern emerges. I get an interview on Monday (though I have to admit I've never obtained a post if there has been another applicant for the job), but within the month the head has usually drawn up some reference for me, couched I must add in glowing terms, an eulogy in fact, to ensure I find employment at some other school – any other school in fact. At one time I spent hours just sitting down wondering why it is I don't fit in in the typical school staff room, but somehow the answer always seems to elude me. OK, so I'm a rustic, a bit down to earth, very down at heel, but while not neat and tidy, I'm not particularly dirty – for a chap who lives in a bachelor hovel, that is. Yet, time and time again I get gently squeezed out of a job and so enthusiastic are the staff about my departure that the quantity of leaving presents – usually dictionaries (perhaps they are trying to tell me something) – would fill a jumble sale in a good-sized church hall.

On the very last day of term the day of my departure from a school, I listen to the head deliver a glowing and breathtaking description of my prowess as a teacher – at least it sounds breathtaking, it could simply be a sigh of relief that I am on my way – and get handed some carefully parcelled presents from staff and kids, but behind the sorry-to-see-you-go look on the head's face, I know full well that he is pleased as punch to watch my mucky van clank out of the school gates for the last time, the very last time at that.

I used to think my eccentric ways alienated the head and staff alike, but hell, I'm not that eccentric, at least not compared to some of the staff with whom I've worked. Yet when the police or the men in white coats gently carry off the real weirdos to incarcerate them where they cannot molest girl, boy, man or in some cases beasts, the heads I've met usually weep genuine tears at the loss of a member of the staff who would have caused some rather odd glances in the zaniest of drooling wards. It's me I guess. I just don't fit in.

Just an example to prove that compared to fellow acceptable teachers in the profession I'm fairly normal. Homosexuals or a variety of multi-coloured sexual deviants, as variable as a box of Smarties, are not uncommon in any profession I suppose, as a glance at the Sunday papers usually indicates all too graphically, and providing a member of the staff of a school isn't too obvious about his little kinks, nothing is said to him or her. Curiously, when I first started teaching not even suede shoes were worn in private between consenting adults, whereas these days a member of the staff blowing up a Billy Connolly joke inflatable sexual doll would scarcely cause a raised eyebrow from staff or kids. I once worked at a school where a very inadequate teacher – the kids gave him sheer hell – obtained his kicks from visiting what the magistrates at his trial described as a 'notorious toilet' (how a toilet can be notorious beats me), boring a hole through the wall and pushing – the rest I'll leave to the reader's imagination – through the wall. Things went well if a person of a similar ilk – I was about to use the term 'bent', but it has a hint of double entendre about it by today's standards – inhabited or was using the next cubicle. Sadly – as they say 'the best laid plans of mice and men' – the poor devil performed his party piece while a happily married carpenter equipped with a bag of hammers was using the next cubicle. The rest is also left to the reader's imagination and I will merely hint at the fact that fate was kind to the poor devil in as much as apparently the carpenter had left his saw on the building site. The head lamented the resignation of this teacher whose habits resembled those of a sex-maddened wood-boring beetle with copious and genuine tears, yet constantly hinted that I should look for pastures which, if not greener, would certainly be newer. Truly I have worked in schools where there was such an incredible incidence of sexual freakos that the head need only have appointed a necrophiliac (check that one in your Shorter Oxford) for him to be able to shout, 'House'. He'd got the whole set of human frailties under one roof. Yet I was always the one to whom the head hinted, 'You've been too long in this town – it's time to move on.' Boy oh boy, by the time I reached forty working in that profession, those heads had given me a force ten inferiority complex and I slunk from school to school wondering what in hell was wrong with me. Well, I was forty and that just about brings the tale level with the story of Nurse Moore and the duck.

I returned to school well-stretched physically, if not mentally, only to find that there had been a timetable reshuffle and, as I was unable to defend myself, I had fairly predictably been phased out. Phasing out is a fairly common practice in the profession – if a group who practise this quaint, unpleasant and nasty little ritual, really deserve the title 'profession'. Perhaps a more accurate noun for a group of teachers who indulge in this nasty little game is a 'clutch' and it now behoves me to explain the analogy.

When a teacher is phased out – it can be for a variety of reasons – it is seldom that he or she is inefficient, the teacher is literally ostracised by the rest of the staff in much the same way as a medieval peasant was ostracised by the rest of the village when he was excommunicated. He or she is given a very sparse timetable, a timetable so full of free time that the teacher not only feels shut off from the rest of the staff, but because the victim is seen not to be 'gainfully employed' incurs a spot more enmity from an already malevolent group. The group now aggravated by the fact that they have a full timetable and the victim has not, respond to the misery of the victim by pecking and hurting as if to satisfy what can almost be called a communal desire to inflict pain and misery. Likewise, a pheasant chick pecked either deliberately or accidentally by one of the group and caused to bleed attracts the rest of the fellow peckers and hurters who peck, rip, rend and tear until the poor chick is no more than a fleshless pulp and a few pieces of oddly angled bone. Hence, I make no excuse for the collective noun 'a clutch of teachers'. I've seen such treatment meted out to others, watched the despair it creates in the victim, noted how the despair degenerated to a state of wretched moral and mental disintegration and finally the broken dispirited member of the staff is forced to resign and perhaps leave teaching and seek an appointment in industry. Then when all is seemingly settled and all that remains is a broken remnant of a human being seething with bitterness, lacking confidence and dwelling in the shadows of the contempt of the rest of the staff, on the last day of term the head pops up and delivers an eulogy on the magnificent qualities of the teacher he has just helped break, and to present him with a present bought with contributions from members of the staff who have assisted in destroying the poor devil. It is, all in all, as false and treacherous as Judas passing his share of the Last Supper across the table to Jesus, but amazingly few members of the staff seem to feel badly about the way they have acted in destroying a colleague and, hey ho, we are into the next term seeking out some other person to hurt, someone else to persecute, someone else to humiliate, to deflate and to mentally destroy.

Just after my spinal injury my own lot became much the same as that of a hundred unfortunates who had been 'smelled out', like the victim of an African witch doctor who seeks to find some scapegoat for some imaginary crime or other. However, my case was just a shade different for I've always been able to control difficult kids, kids with a flare for creating mayhem, and as many staff tend to go sick when given a surfeit of these classes, I spent my time filling in for such teachers. It was a demoralising month or so as perhaps it was intended to be, and predictably, I found myself going into the usual depressive nosedive, out of which I found it impossible to pull back. I was heading for the dole queue, and fast, for a forty-year-old teacher with no other skills is literally on one's BTM job prospect-wise. I racked my brains to think of any skills I had acquired apart from being able to teach – I was still convinced I was good in the classroom. I knew I was, but I had no manual dexterity and the more I thought about my plight the more convinced I was that I was going quietly nuts. The state of depression hit the pits, so to speak, when I chanced on a dead rabbit on the edge of a roundabout called Muckly Corner, and seeing pieces of the cadaver dispersed by passing cars, each one tearing a minute piece of meat off the poor devil, made me envy the lot of the beast. The rabbit was out of his misery but I had another day of boredom to face, another week maybe, even a year of suffering, a feeling of uselessness and perhaps that moment marked the most unhappy spot of my life – at least I hope it did, I just couldn't take another beating like the one I took that year.

Funnily enough, the word 'beating' brings me to the next part of my tale, for I went to the fights at Wolverhampton Civic Hall that night to watch a boy I had trained and sponsored make his professional debut. I suppose it would be a lie to say that such places are choc-a-bloc with savants or places to seek out and find men of infinite wisdom, but it is equally untrue to imagine that the boxing scene is full of Damyon Runyon type down-and-outs and punch-drunk pugs mumbling always inarticulately, 'Give me a chance, Mr Schmerkil, I'm ready to make a come back'. In fact, come to think of it, I've learned a hell of a lot about life from my contact with the professional fight scene, and I was about to be taught even more of the no-holds-barred, sod-the-Marquis-of-Queensbury game called 'Life', that very night.

I sat next to Michael Kahn, a well over the top but once useful amateur fighter who claimed, and I believe him, that he had been taught the skills of the toughest game in the world by Jimmy Wilde, a six-stone chunk of manhood who became world flyweight champion in the early days of the century, and who in spite of his frail physique, downed a huge batch of worthies who out-weighed him by up to four stones or more.

I sat chattering to Michael, idly making small talk as one does just before the start of a big fight, waiting for the lights to dim and the gladiators to be announced – young babes shimmering with vitality and hope, each one dreaming of becoming a world champion, each one convinced of his own immortality and indestructibility. I'd been like this once, I mused, and now I was a shabby, down-at-heel dispirited forty-year-old with no prospects, no future and what was worse, no hope or wish to live. I looked up and found Kahn's craggy face studying me carefully. He had a peculiar wisdom, the sort of wisdom that comes ready-packaged at birth and isn't blunted by formal education. I've met his kind many times and it's amazing the common sense a man can pick up in a twenty-four foot square ring.

'Something's wrong, isn't it?' he said.

Forthwith I blurted out my problems, desperate perhaps to have someone who would listen to my lament. He sat and listened patiently as the hall filled slowly and silently for the fight crowd are a far cry from football hooligans. I came to the end of my lament desperately and almost breathlessly.

'Are you sure you are any good as a teacher?' he asked, almost cautiously.

'Yes, Mike, I'm good. No, I'm bloody good. I'm just getting a very rough deal and I'm damned if I can see a way out of it. There doesn't seem a damned thing I can do to fight the system.'

'Is your boy second on the bill?' he asked, changing the subject suddenly.

I nodded disappointedly perhaps at the fact that the advice I'd sought, or maybe expected, wasn't forthcoming. He studied his programme, perhaps just a little too carefully I now realise on reflection.

'The boy your lad's up against is . . . dirty – apt to foul if he can?'.

Again I nodded.

'What would you do if your boy was repeatedly fouled by this guy, and the ref seemingly did nothing?'

I thought only for a moment before answering. The answer was obvious and standard practice in the square ring.

'Obviously I'd get my lad to pull his opponent to the centre of the ring so that everyone could see he was being fouled.'

I think he studied my face a second or so before replying, perhaps wondering why I'd learned so little about life from my stint in the square ring.

'Don't you think that perhaps you're fighting your enemies the wrong way?' he said softly, and as if nothing had been said, no superb advice given, this man with the wisdom of Nestor, returned to the programme and added, 'Fifth on the bill, looks a tidy bout', and at that the lights dimmed and the contests began.

He had in a few words given me more advice than any solicitor could have drummed up in a £500 afternoon session. I watched my boy snatch a hard-won victory, shook hands with Kahn, and drove my fighter home listening to his excited, wildly exuberant account of the battle which seemed to be quite a different fight from the one I'd just watched. Elation at success in young fighters is one of the few perks of the fight game for the purses are pitifully small, and that night the lad could scarcely claim that he had my undivided attention.

I went to school next day a manic surge raging through my body and penned a letter asking to be reassessed by the Department of Education and Science, and for an interview with the Director of Education, to which I intended to bring a friend from the press rather than my union representative, as is the custom in the seemingly highly correct world of teaching. I knew full well that what I had done was an unprecedented move, certain to cause consternation at the education office, controversy with the powers that were, and a hell of a lot of bad publicity for the profession, but as I reflected I really had absolutely nothing to lose, and after my talk with Kahn I was really psyched up and raring to go, even if I had a fifteen-round battle to fight. I was also determined not to emulate the sad fate of those I'd seen who didn't fit in, that I'd seen whimper and whine into resignation or early retirement with a life of penury on a pitiful breadline pension. I had no fears about my ability to endure an inspection for at college I'd been a star turn, though I confess it had been a hurry-on-down situation since then, but I was still good enough to appear somethng special if the Department of Education and Science did send an honest and competent inspector to reassess me. A flurry of letters came to me from those in power, but I knew that what I had done had caused those who were deliberately making my life a misery to 'run scared' as they say in ring terminology. No school dare chance publicity of the kind I had planned, and once the press get their knives into anything to do with education, a whole load of skeletons fall out of a whole load of cupboards and a mess is dredged up which makes the bottom of the cesspit seem like a sterilised operating room. So I was reinstated, given a timetable of sorts, but the whole messy business was a hollow victory and left a bitter taste in my mouth.

I suppose it could be said that I tottered through the next year aware of the fact that the stunt I'd pulled was a one-off job never to be repeated and that I was living on borrowed time. That week I resolved to seek new employment – any job in fact which would allow me to slip the fetters of teaching. That week I really buckled down to hard work and penned my first book. I'd made the first tentative steps to get out of teaching, but it was to be some time before I finally plucked up courage and slipped the chain.

GOLDEN EAGLE

—3—

Running Away

COME TO THINK of it it's not just teachers I dislike. I'm not very keen on the human race generally and I have the oddest feeling that the Almighty looking down on us must shrug his Sistine Chapel type shoulders, stroke his grey beard – which if one is logical about it should not really be grey – and murmur,'Oh well, this batch is a failure. Suppose I strike up a Model II using silicon rather than carbon as a base. Verily, as a biological experiment mankind can hardly be classed as a success story – not by a long chalk.'

Curiously, being ostracised by society gives a man the advantage of being able to stand back and watch the human race with an almost detached attitude, and because I am able to do this simply because I have been frequently ostracised, I am aware that what I see is nothing to admire and certainly nothing to envy or emulate. At one time I worked at a school in Rotherham where one of the dominant harridans used to remark, 'Don't you wish you were normal?' I became self-conscious about comments like these and perhaps during my early and middle twenties when my eccentricities were beginning to manifest themselves, I did wish I was normal. However, on examining what the rest of mankind considered normal, I suppose I opted out, not only of the rat race but of society generally, and when the going gets a bit rough and the expected or conventional becomes nasty and unpleasant, I still opt out. Now more than half-way through my forties, I own (together with The Royal Bank of Scotland I must add) a tiny croft near John O'Groats, and when the world begins to 'crowd' me, and people get on top of me, I take off there and sit out the inner storm, the unbearable misery, I've probably generated through my own peculiarities. Before I had the croft, I just roughed it for a few weeks, sleeping rough, and eating even rougher – 'living dirty' one of my sisters once called it. OK so running away from life is cowardly. Well, perhaps I am a coward but by having a panic snap clip I could release at will, I've kept, if not sane, at least not 'committable' as they say in the Midlands.

My duel with the school powers over, I had only a brief spell to recover before the whole world ganged up again and I found myself in my usual muddled, 'hell-of-a-mess' condition. Bills had piled up during my depressive state when nothing seems to get done, and now County Court orders mingled happily with Final Demand letters on the doormat in my porch. I fell foul of a local councillor – and boy oh boy, do such people have powers in the Midlands – and he began to make life hell. Smartly dressed, perplexed and often embarrassed public health officers would arrive to enquire why I had a full kennel of dogs and no breeder's licence (most of the bitches were geriatric), or I'd get planning officers around with clipboards and notes just 'looking over' my shack. Well, being a macho kind of person, I did the only thing I could. I ran away. I phoned Ian Bullock, a lad in my class who could be trusted – dates me a bit as he now owns IB Field Sports – and arranged for him to look after the dogs for a week or so while I went into hiding and, bundling Penguin and her daughter Fathom into the back of my filthy van together with a suitcase full of seen-better-days clothes, I set off for – well, just about anywhere. As I switched on the van ignition – a curious piece of equipment which rather defies the physical laws that electricity travels at near on the speed of light, for it took about eight seconds for the light to go on – a callow youth appeared at the door of my house, book in hand.

'Will you sign my book for me?' he asked, proferring a copy of *Lurchers and Long Dogs* by Ted Walsh. I shook my head in despair, finally signing the book Guy N. Smith, leaving the youth happy and content. Well, I'll say this much for good old homo sapiens – as a species he may not be up to much, but he's easily satisfied, too easily perhaps. The van fired first time, a good omen and I travelled through Walsall to the M6. I flipped a coin and it came down north, so north is was, along the dreariest length of road designed by man. North, but nowhere in particular north, not giving a damn where I was heading, where I stayed, or how in hell the meagre sum of money in my bank account, and the thirty-five pounds in my pocket, would sustain me. Exhaust clanking and lights sort of flickering on the dashboard, I set out on the totally irrational task of hiding from the world. I knew the road well enough, as months before I'd started work on a book called *Fell Terriers*, so from Walsall to Carlisle through Holmes Chapel was well explored and fairly well known. Dusk began to fall as a sign for Kendal began to loom on the horizon, and for a while I did consider hiding out in the Lake District. However, the thoughts of bright young things, embryonic success-story students, all clad in orange cagoules, tramping the hills quoting Wordsworth, put me off and I headed north towards Carlisle.

My van began to jib, to vary the frequency of its shudders, as we came near Shap, picking up damp I suppose for Shap always seems covered in a fine mist. My problems, indeed my whole life, becomes insignificant when I come face to face with an area such as Shap – a huge granite mound which had pushed its way from the earth's centre causing the hills to dome and buckle.

At the top of Shap, miles from the nearest turn-off, I saw a figure walking along the hard shoulder of the motorway, hitching a lift. I make it a rule to always give hitch-hikers a ride quite simply because if I do a good turn for someone else, they'll pass it on and logically it goes straight around the world and comes back to me. That's how it goes in theory anyway – somehow it gets lost, very lost, long before it gets back to me. Still it's a great philosophy, shame it doesn't work! However, a fine drizzle of the sort that wets one right through to the bone was falling, and it would have been a hard-hearted driver who would pass by the sodden figure, collar up to keep out the worst of the drizzle, who stood on that bleak area of the motorway hoping to get a lift. So, much as I hate the company of people when I'm on a depressive nosedive, I slowed up my van to a clanking halt, pushed Penguin and Fathom off the front seat and offered the poor sodden traveller a lift. On reflection I'm glad I did, but likewise perhaps it would have been better if I had driven on and given the pleasure of his company to another motorist with a similar liking for hitch-hikers.

The door opened and a man in his mid-twenties perhaps, maybe a shade older, literally leaped in.

'Flick the heater on, mate,' said a voice that was a mix of a strong Scottish accent mingled with what I took to be an Irish brogue.

The courtesy light revealed a man with an Asiatic-type face, Mongoloid, would perhaps best describe him.

'God, this seat is warm,' he said, nestling into the warmth left by the two dogs. 'Warm to the arse,' he added, a little less poetically.

'Where's you going?' asked the Mongoloid-looking chap, rubbing his face to restore circulation and shaking his black, greasy locks until the van was showered with water and a few less pleasant things.

'I'm not quite sure where,' I said, rather sheepishly, feeling more than a little foolish, 'but I'm heading North.'

'Suits me, suits me fine,' replied the young buck and introduced himself, 'Jamie, Jamie McPhee,' he added warmly.

Thus one Jamie McPhee became my uninvited guide to Scotland as we bypassed Carlisle and journeyed to Glasgow, van rattling, heater blowing a sort of oily hot air into the already smelly cab.

Whenever my thoughts stray back to that long and tedious journey, the adjective 'garrulous' always comes to mind for Jamie talked non-stop. There's a tribe in South America (well, at least according to W. H. Hudson's book *Green Mansions* there is), where a man is admired and a boy literally undergoes his tribal 'barmitzvah' simply by talking the sun around – a full non-stop, twenty-four-hour babble; your choice of subject. By the time we reached the café on the outskirts of Glasgow, I was convinced that not only was Jamie a member of that tribe (hence the very unBritish features), but that he had either devised the ceremony or passed it with flying colours. He paused for breath a moment as we rattled into the car park of the café.

'Der MacPhees is the oldest tribe in Scotland.'

I nodded. I'd bought an antique edition of McIan's book of the Scottish clans and it seemed likely that the Pictish people, the earliest Celtic settlers of Scotland, were dark of skin and perhaps Jamie was a descendant of one of these people; the sort that unhappy Roman soldiers stationed on the Antonine Wall wrote home and complained about. Pict is a derivation of Pictii, the painted people, as the natives were supposed to paint designs on their faces and naked bodies in a blue dye made from a plant called woad.

'You don't look Scottish,' I said, immediately aware of the sheer stupidity of the statement – how in hell could anyone look Scottish?

'Naw,' Jamie replied. 'We, der McPhees dat is, was from shipwrecked Japanese sailors who was washed up on the Pentland Firth.'

I was about to ask him how he reconciled this tale with the statement that he was from one of the oldest tribes in Scotland, but a burly-looking, red-haired lorry driver standing behind us in the queue, leading to the self-service hatch, began to take umbrage that we weren't moving quickly enough and so, discretion ever being the better part of valour, Jamie and I moved on quickly to be served, leaving most of his supposed genealogy unexplored. I'd worked out that I could afford egg, chips and tea, as we neared the hatch. I ordered, watching Jamie's face also scanning the board.

'I haddna eaten all day,' he added, his Mongoloid face developing an incongruous Oliver Twist look.

I groaned, sighed and finally gave in.

'OK, what do you want?'

Quick as a flash he went the whole hog, ordering a £3.75 meal with melon to follow. I paid up silently but bitterly, tears nearly dampening my eyes and we sat eating our meals – Jamie for the first time silent – in the far corner of the café. He wolfed down his food quickly and I was about to say rather petulantly that it was the first time I'd seen sparks generated by a knife and fork, when he finished his meal, slammed down his cutlery as if they were red hot – they probably were – and announced he was buying some Mars Bars as if the statement had some momentous significance. (Indeed, as I later discovered, every time Jamie actually paid for anything out of his own money it was an act of momentous significance.) I was about to reach into my pocket and hand him a hard-earned fifty pence piece when he whipped out a bundle of fivers, big enough to choke a horse, and strode to the confectionery section. I watched him literally swallow a few bars whole before he returned to me, brushing flakes of chocolate from the corner of his mouth.

'You bastard,' I exploded. 'You bloody bastard.'

'Yer didna ask if I had money to pay for the meal,' he uttered as if amazed at my outburst.

But by that time I was well aware that Jamie was a professional conman who probably 'palmed' his way around the country fleecing every 'lift' he was given until they 'wised up' to his game, and Jamie was probably well used to my offensive expletive about the circumstances of his parentage. I suppose a professional cadger – and Jamie was a professional cadger – must regard the fury of the 'mark' (sucker) he has just hit, as an occupational hazard or maybe an added pleasure. He seemed not the slightest bit offended.

'Where we off now?' he asked as if nothing had been said, and followed me out to the van snatching a huge pack of McEwan's Bitter from the counter and secreting it under his still damp jacket.

'You're a thief as well as a cadger,' I said contemptuously.

'Yes,' he replied.

He opened the van door and got inside, though the stench emitted from Penguin and Fathom who lay in the back of the van would have deterred a homeless skunk. It was, so it seemed, impossible to offend Jamie – and before the end of the journey I'd tried hard enough, believe me.

We bypassed Glasgow, heading for the A82, or come to think of it, anywhere where I could dislodge my unwelcome companion, who seemed to cling to me like a limpet. I began to long to hear his dulcet tones utter, 'I get off here', but seemingly where I was going Jamie was going.

'If yer not going anywhere particular like, I'd go south – der's history there. D'you like history? I hate history,' he added hopefully.

I shrugged my shoulders, indicating that I had but a casual interest in history, aware that he was offering his services as a guide though Dumfries and Galloway with the possibility of a free meal or so thrown in at an all-night Wigtown café. My silence or reluctance to say Yea or Nay unzipped Jamie's garrulous mouth yet once more and he came out with a quasi-historial spiel that would have put Baron Munchausen, the world's greatest liar, to shame. It was such an incredible off-course tale that for a moment I wondered if Jamie wrote Open University text books when he wasn't begging free meals from lift-giving marks.

A fine drizzle had started to fall as we drove around the convoluted ring roads which surround Glasgow, and as the lazy windscreen wipers made half-hearted attempts to clear the windscreen, Jamie began his travelogue, attempting to lapse out of his Irish-Scottish limbo dialect and affect a BBC English accent as if to add extra value to the tale.

'Many years ago – a hundred million years ago, no, two hundred million years,' he threw in for good measure, 'dese parts was inhabited by two tribes called der Shamrocks and der Young Young Shamrocks. Very fierce people indeed,' he put in. 'Very fierce indeed,' he bit his lip at the memory of their ferocity. I nearly choked with laughter and my endeavour to suppress my mirth caused me to splutter and cough. The Shamrocks and the Young Young Shamrocks were a group of toughs – or perhaps not so toughs – who supported the football teams, Celtic and Rangers, and only appeared as if by elfin magic on the days just before the Cup Final or in the days after the said match, when they admittedly did create mayhem, though scarcely the mayhem created by elfin-type folk. I had the oddest feeling that either Jamie's history teacher was football crazy or simply a micky-taking alcoholic, who was taking out his bitterness at being rejected as a Monty Python script writer. Jamie, undeterred by my coughing and spluttering mirth went on, 'Dey was always fighting de Irish', and here my guide came a little nearer to the truth than he imagined, and reader, steal yourself for a quick history lesson which I'll make as quick as possible and try not to be boring.

I suppose everyone in Britain, Jamie included, has heard of Hadrian's Wall, a vast piece of ineffectual construction built across country parallel to the River Tyne at certain parts, which apparently served two purposes. Firstly the wall was built at the time of the Emperor Hadrian (which seems logical as it was called Hadrian's Wall) to keep back raiding tribes of Scottish folk from invading England and committing the usual atrocities one associates with Vandals, Vikings and Liverpool Football Club supporters – and in this function one must add it failed miserably – and secondly to enable parties of visiting school kids to complain bitterly that there is 'no bloody wall to be seen, just mounds of sodding earth', and to ask for their money back. In the second function the wall, one must add, was an unprecedented success for I have yet to meet a coach party of kids returning from the said wall who weren't in a state of rebellion about paying a coach fare to see 'a mound of bloody earth and a few stones'.

Come to think of it, from the laying of the first stone, Hadrian's Wall seemed to be a loser and so the Romans, a dauntless race no matter what World War II veterans say about the Italians in general, marched even further north to the Firth of Forth and built yet another wall to keep back the Scottish tribes (and provide further ammunition for parties of school kids to claim that 'education is a rip off' – perhaps more so as the Antonine Wall was built of earth clods not stones and only archaeologists with a tile or so loose bother digging around these, although I suppose it does provide incontroversial evidence that at one time there really was a Roman in the gloaming).

The Romans, hardy race or not, complained bitterly about the damp climate and were treated rather badly by the Scottish tribes about whom they wrote home bitter letters, lying about the ferocity of the tribes and the savage barbarism of the Pictish people in the same manner as 'Virgin Soldiers' serving in Malaya wrote home about the ferocity of the sixteen-year-old Chinese terrorists they were fighting. Some really weird tales permeated into Rome – one of which was that the Pictish Scots were feeble by day, but came to life with a vengeance by night – a fact I can well bear out about the Scots I met while I worked for Wimpeys, who were a bit sluggish on the hods by day but were hellers after opening time. (The next bit is hard to follow, but reader stick with me, as all will be revealed.) However, some time during Roman times – I'm a scientist not a historian – an Irish tribe called ironically the Scots invaded Pictland which is now called Scotland and thus gave Scotland its name. I tried to explain this to Jamie as well, but he didn't understand either, and rather than persist with the explanation I agreed with him that historians were probably a band of nutters and that the original dwellers probably were called Shamrocks and Young Young Shamrocks. Perhaps I give up easily but I could tell at a glance Jamie was hardly likely to benefit from my knowledge, give up his shiftless cadging life and become an academic or a historian with a dedication to authentic Scottish history.

Anyway Jamie was well and truly off history by this time and was well and truly onto a rather nasty little biological discourse on the effect the cans of stolen McEwan's Bitter were having on his intestinal functions, particularly in the early part of the morning. Nevertheless, he continued to quaff the stuff by the canful, and I made a mental note to be well rid of him before the first rays of light, which not only enfeebled the Picts but also made Jamie a little less than pleasant as a travelling companion – even in my evil-smelling van.

The McEwan's Bitter, despite Jamie's claim that it had gut-destroying properties, kept Jamie's garrulous tongue well and truly oiled and he continued with his history lessons.

'Pity yer not going south,' he uttered twixt belches and complaints about gastric pains, eager to have one last stab at getting me to change direction. 'Cos they eat people in Galloway. Well, they used to', he paused a moment as if to recall one of his historical seminars no doubt, 'till the last war in 1963.' I remarked that this was probably one of the very best reasons for going north, as in Scotland old habits, such as eating people, die hard, but whereas Jamie was a bit out of touch date-wise, I had a rough idea what he meant.

In 1774, a down-on-his-luck writer called George Wilkinson became one of the first to realise that what the reading public wanted were not volumes about morality, good living and the benefits of a pure soul, but books about crime, more crime and snippets of horror thrown in for good measure, and a spot of sexual atrocity if any could be found. Hence, Wilkinson concocted a whole load of stories about the escapist Jack Shepherd, the villainous thief-taker Jonathan Wilde, and that's all I know about these two apart from the fact I've seen *Where's Jack?* starring Tommy Steele and Stanley Baker, as the respective heinous villains. However, interesting as these two villains were, Wilkinson, out to start the book with a bang, came up with the story of stories which guaranteed his readership, for he came up with the tale of one Sawney Bean – a story certain to whet one's appetite, which on reflection may be an unfortunate turn of phrase. Bean, a man of somewhat curious and gluttonous eating habits, was omnivorous to a degree seldom encountered these days. He married a near-imbecile woman – well, at least that's what Wilkinson says – and the happy couple went off on honeymoon looking for someone to rob, maim or kill. The first victim of their month of marital bliss that they happened to kill (well, it makes a change from non-stop sex) was found to be penniless, so according to Wilkinson, the Beans who were desperately upset at the apparent state of penury of the wretch they had just killed, were at their wits' end deciding what to do with the cadaver. The Beans, however, were an inventive family and it was agreed that they would eat him – no, you haven't missed a page – eat him. Once the victim was devoured, the Beans set out on a life of crime, but apparently human morsels are as addictive as heroin, for once the Beans had acquired a taste for human meat there was literally no holding them, and they set about gobbling up the population of Galloway which didn't please the King's tax gatherer much and I don't suppose the natives of Galloway liked it all that much either. The Beans produced a family who mated wildly and incestuously according to Prest, who wrote a book about the nasty little family, producing wild and near-mad children, all with a yen for human meat, and giving rise to a really sick joke about Mrs Bean, who after enjoying a spot of illicit naughty with her eldest son says, 'You do this better than your father does.' To which Bean junior replies, 'Yes, that's what my sister says.' Personally I doubt if the joke has foundation in fact, but according to Wilkinson within less than thirty years there were some forty-eight nasty little Beans with incestuous leanings, and a ready answer to the council estate complainant who says, 'Do you know, I just don't know what to make of my neighbours.'

Well, once more, to cut a long story short, the Beans succeeded in literally cleaning out Galloway of edible folk, and, to cut an even longer story shorter, James I of Scotland was holding court near Galloway when a chap burst in claiming that a band of naked people had attacked his wife who was riding pillion – horseback not motor bike I hasten to add, as it was 1405 when these sundry nasties were supposed to have happened – pulled her off the horse and started eating her. Now even by the standards of the time – border raiders and all that – this was a fairly unusual tale and well worth looking into. So James, plus a company of soldiers promptly sought out the Beans and found the whole family seated around in a cave in which there were sides of people smoked like bacon for the Beans were a careful family and made provision for a wet and unproductive Midlothian winter. The King, however, took a rather dim view of the Beans's housekeeping or cavekeeping (call it what you will) and in 1405 he executed the whole family, separating the males from the females – a hint of Scottish prudery perhaps – and after chopping off the genitals of the males he burned the whole lot, males, females and genitalia on three separate fires, which seemed a rather curious, absurd and rather an effort-wasting exercise, but then I'm not a Scot and I suppose times were different then.

Later a chap called Thomas Prescott Prest picked up the tale and wrote a spine-chilling trilogy called *Varney, the Vampire* (more daft than horrific, if you ask me), *Sawney Bean, the Man Eater of Midlothian*, and surpassed himself with an epic of cannibalism called *Sweeny Todd, the Demon Barber*, who not only 'did in' his victims under the pretext of shaving them, but also did unspeakable things to the deceased, selling them as pie filling – an unlikely tale I suppose but then a story which smacked of realism just as much as James I's curious three-fire trick. I checked on Prest and found not only did Varney not exist – it would be a shade unlikely if a bona fide vampire had, though looking at the bites on Rosie's neck (my class monitor), I felt it needed checking – but there is no evidence to suggest that neither Sweeny or Sawney Bean did either. Pity they make a nice tale.

A lorry coming in the opposite direction illuminated the cab of my van, and I glanced across at Jamie to tell him of the Sawney Bean myth. He lay there asleep, Mars Bar smearing his gaping mouth, and a tiny trickle of a hybrid mix of spittle and McEwan's running down his chin, staining his already messy sweater with a compendium of Inverness and Slough products. He belched and a foul odour filled the van. I shook my head in disbelief.

'This is a fine mess you've got me into, Stanley,' I said to myself more than McPhee.

'Aye, aye,' in his McEwan's-induced sleep he uttered, treating me to another quick belch.

I pulled off the road and wound down both windows and slept until morning, cold but fairly free from gastric odours.

SLED DOG

—4—

Out of Place, Out of Time

I AWOKE COLD and stiff to find Jamie vomiting copiously out of the passenger window of the van.

'Oh Christ, no, Oh Christ,' he muttered, wiping the foul mess with the back of his hand.

'I shall not pick up hitch-hikers again,' I said quietly.

'Yer right,' said Jamie. 'There's some right foul weirdees on the road,' and poured another can of McEwan's down his throat to wash down another rapidly crammed-in Mars Bar.

'You're a vile, nauseating pig of a person, a disgusting animal, Jamie,' I spat out venomously.

'Yeh, yer right, yer dead right,' he muttered, too sick and ill to disagree with my attack on his character and disposition, or perhaps he even agreed with my analysis.

In contempt for my travelling companion, I turned the ignition key a little too hard perhaps, and the engine spluttered, kicked and died, picking up again with a roaring sound. We shuddered north again on the road which led into the ill-fated valley of Glencoe, scene of an incident too well recorded to be mentioned by an amateur historian such as myself. The road leading to Glencoe is, at least in mid-winter, perhaps one of the most bleak and depressing roads in Britain, and the cold light of dawn and my puking, evil-smelling travelling companion did little to alleviate the misery of the trip.

I drove on in silence feeling very dirty, unshaven and unwashed, and on inhaling deeply, aware that Jamie must have bathed every six months whether he needed it or not. From time to time I cast a glance at him and became gleefully aware of divine justice. God is not blind and savagely punishes those who nick McEwan's Bitter from transport cafés, though, I admit, there's nothing in Leviticus about it. Jamie's face had turned an even dirtier grey and he was becoming more ill by the second as he darted his head out of the window, uttering such cryptic epigrams as, 'Better out than in', and several other sayings probably much beloved by persistent drunkards, and those who regularly regurgitate out of the windows of moving vans. I averted my gaze, feeling self-righteous and smug at the plight and physical condition of my travelling companion. Verily, thou shalt not steal from the counters of transport cafés! With a look of contempt, a sort of general contempt for human frailty which most teachers seem to acquire within months of leaving college and never to lose until retirement, I glanced out of the side window of the van at an earth track leading up into the mountains. The grey daylight revealed what I first thought to be an apparition, and I had to stare hard to believe that what I thought I saw was actually happening. Out of the mists which still hung around the tops of the hills, I saw a man riding a platformed vehicle chasing four medium-sized dogs, and though the man was going lickety-spit on his platform, he seemed not to be gaining on the dogs, and while it was apparent that they too were going all-out the dogs seemed unable not only to shake off their pursuer nor even to pull away from him. I nudged my travelling companion who grunted awake.

'Yeh,' he belched.

'Jamie, look at that,' I said, pointing at the dogs and pursuer who seemed to disappear from time to time as the path was shielded from view by high banks only to reappear again, the dogs maintaining exactly the same lead as before.

Jamie had nodded off to sleep again, groaning softly, lamenting the evils of the Inverness Brewery Company, so I punched him a little too hard perhaps in the ribs.

'Look,' I repeated.

He belched from the force of the blow and glanced across not remotely interested in the spectacle.

'Yeh,' he yawned. 'It's a daft bugger.'

At the time I thought Jamie knew all about what was happening, though it later transpired he referred to anyone he didn't agree with or understand, and which incidentally included most of the human race, as 'a daft bugger'. I can remember nodding as if in agreement with Jamie's comment, for such a spectacle staged on a remote Scottish hillside in the early hours of the morning made me feel as though I had travelled through a torn curtain into one of the oddball worlds of Jonathan Swift or Michael Moorcock or perhaps been allowed a last-minute peep at the academy for the insane at Brigadoon. The cavalcade seemed to pull up near a huge van which was parked some twenty yards up the dirt track off the main road, and it would have been an iron-willed man who could have driven on without inspecting the curiosity he had just watched and obtaining at least an explanation or even a further glance. I am not such a man, and I turned the van up the path to where the large red American-type Dormobile-cum-homestead was parked.

A tall well-built man in his mid-thirties perhaps (it is difficult to decide about most untypical people), was engaged in uncoupling a team of sled-type dogs from a line connected to a platform which, steered by a bar, was attached to the stanchion of the platform. He noticed, glanced up, sighed a little, shrugged his shoulders and went back to work, calming down his team of dogs which seemed totally oblivious to my presence and screamed and barked as if eager to be pulling that curious contraption again.

I stopped and watched, head to one side as I am wont to do when I find something totally beyond my comprehension taking place, and almost felt the uneasiness of the man uncoupling the dogs. At last he could stand it no longer and turned to me.

'Can I help you?' he asked, in a cultured perhaps mid-Atlantic accent of the sort sported by English DJs from Keswick to Kensington. 'Can I help you, sir?' he asked again with a Rhett Butler lilt.

I was about to answer, 'No', but I realised the comment would have seemed ridiculous as, 'Dr Livingstone I presume'.

'I'm just interested in what you are doing, that's all,' I mumbled, a little shamefacedly.

He shrugged his shoulders and went back to work on the frenzied leaping dogs as if awaiting my next inane comment. He did not have long to wait.

It's at times like these when I become aware of the extent of my own ignorance. I had been reared on a diet of Jack London books, bed-fellows of well-thumbed copies of *Das Capital*, my father's books stored in an old tin trunk in my bedroom and used as 'read aloud' books in my abortive attempts to cure my fearful stammer, an affliction which still reappears when I am upset by even trivial incidents. By my tenth birthday magical names like Dawson, Skagways, Anchorage, Nome, Sitka, Pelee, rang in my head and while the rest of the village lads romanced about being Stanley Matthews, I saw myself amidst blinding snow and ice, mushing a team of ill-tamed wolves, gaunt hunger-maddened McKenzie River huskies, across a bleak and windy tundra. My colleagues, fellow travellers, half-bred Frenchmen, wild and lawless as their dogs, speaking a mishmash of French, English and Norwegian, but the Solleks, the Dub, the Dave, and the Spitz of Jack London's *Call of the Wild* were huge, larger-than-life hounds, more lupine than canine, recalcitrant as mules unless whipped or thrashed to submission, and a far cry from the screaming, howling little banshees the stranger was uncoupling and preparing to put into the brassy, extrovert, custom-built American-type van.

At last I found my tongue.

'I thought huskies were bigger than those,' I said, nodding across at the wolf-grey lead dog which was scarcely larger than a collie.

The stranger turned slightly, even the all-consuming word 'huskies', touching a nerve perhaps and making him wonder if he'd been correct in assessing the open-mouthed intruder, the brash and inquisitive intruder, into his patently private world, as a complete idiot.

'There are lots of types of huskies, most, if not all, of which are bigger than these. Why, are you interested?'

I was about to mention that not only did all dogs interest me and pompously boast that I had been commissioned to write a book on working terriers, but suddenly the whole puny and pathetic microcosm of my own world seemed piteously unimportant and trivial compared to the world of this man.

'Yes, very,' I finally replied a bit inanely, and seconds later I was glad I had for before leaving my newly acquired friend I had added a new slab of interest to what other members of the teaching staff of my school had called my 'fund of very useless knowledge'.

No better combination can be found than an enthusiast with time on his hands, and a will to impart his knowledge, coupled with an equally willing but totally ignorant newcomer with just about the same amount of time on his hands and just about the same amount of interest in the subject. In such learning situations the knowledge one gleans is literally incredible. Tragically few school kids are motivated by men of this American's ilk. So from the start he explained where, or at least where cynologists (those with a scientific interest in dogs and their origins and history), believe it all started.

In early times man domesticated a type of jackal, so Lorenz and a few others believe – not all cynologists one must add – and by the time early man had entrenched himself in Asia he seems to have bred out the unbearably pungent anal glands of the golden jackal and produced what must have resembled the typical council estate cur. 'Turf dogs', archaeologists call them. In fact, cynologists (that word again) experimenting with unrestricted mongrel breeding, using dogs from unwanted homes have succeeded in producing a murky yellow-brown beast strangely level in type despite its mixed origin and variable genes. These primitive turf dogs were used as warning dogs – they were scarcely big enough to be truly guard dogs – and as hunting companions, for man had not yet progressed far enough along the road to what some might call civilisation, to keep herds of food animals. Some of these tribes moved north into the freezing tundra and beyond into the barrens, and here so dog scientists (I can't use cynologist yet again) believe, the cur dogs hybridised with palaearctic wolves and produced a type of dog which not only looked unlike the jackal-type dogs, but even lacked the subservient eager-to-please nature of the dogs from further south. They returned to their owners when they wished, not immediately they were called, and hunted ahead rather than remaining close to their human companions. As a type they were ideally suited to the environment for their hunting instincts were so finely developed that once the buds on the tundra aspen and birch quickened, and a lightning-quick spring and summer arrived, the dogs ceased to hang around the camps and simply moved out into the barrens hunting their own meat, breeding a litter of puppies now that the warmer more clement days and extra daylight brought the bitches into season. When autumn came, the dogs were hard-pressed for food and returned home to the camp sites of man with whatever puppies chose to associate with men while the rest who cowered beyond the flickering camp fires either died off when winter threatened or became absorbed into the wolf packs as had the dam of Jack London's *White Fang*.

For some reason, and I confess I'm still not happy about the wolf hybrid theory, the progeny of these northern dogs developed a voluminous curled tail, the tip of which resided in the centre of the back and hung loose only when the dogs were out of condition. In addition to these qualities they became frugal eaters with extra-long guts and a more efficient digestive system which extracted the very last morsel of nourishment from food, even staying alive by eating the old leather shoes of their owners. Gradually various types began to emerge. The natives of Central Siberia, the Samoyed, not only produced a hunting/sledding type dog, but sometime in the history of the natives, succeeded in domesticating reindeer, and as herding is only a sublimated hunting instinct, some of the more biddable of the wild and woolly dogs took to herding as well as hunting. In eastern Siberia a tribe which had qualities and an appearance midway between the Mongols and the Eskimos, known as the Chukchi, also domesticated the reindeer, yet apparently never succeeded in developing herding dogs. Indeed, some of the wildest dogs in the world, some of the most intractable stock worriers, came out of this region – dogs which literally refused to become totally domesticated, hunting in packs throughout the summer months, completely unbiddable, refusing to come, particularly if on a scent or worse still in sight of quarry. These dogs must have been dangerous to a tribe which lived permanently on the meat-line rather than on the bread-line, as they were completely unbreakable to stock. These Siberian dogs, or Siberian huskies as they are now called, are an amazing breed and this reluctance to tolerate, let alone accept, livestock is borne out by the fact that puppies raised with the family cat will suddenly for no apparent reason, kill the cat when their owner is looking the other way or has popped out for coffee during a TV break. Chickens and, horror of horror, sheep are usually exterminated on sight, and when on the rampage, a Siberian husky behaves in such a manner as to rival or even excel a rampaging stoat in a pheasant coup. Ten years ago the breed was relatively unknown in Britain, now it is very popular and found not only at dog shows and at sled dog rallies but also as a family pet. However, it is a brave and nerve-free person who keeps this breed as a pet dog, for once off the leash and loose the dog decides when to return and no amount of shouting, pleading or tears can induce the beast to come to hand and return until it is good and ready, and before it is good and ready it usually has ample opportunity to behave like a canine edition of a Manchester United supporter. Still, the breed is a fascinating one and its followers are in all probability as wrapped up in the history of the breed as they are in the dogs themselves.

About 3500 years ago, man, particularly Asiatic man, developed a curious need to migrate. Lots of reasons are put forward for the sudden urge to shift territory. Some believe the invention of the cooking pot enabled man to boil out the ptomaine and salmonella bacteria from food and with food poisoning reduced, if not eliminated, the population literally shot up. Perhaps this population boom triggered off the 'migrations' which were to follow, or perhaps at certain times in man's history a desire to find out what lies beyond the next hill is borne in all men. Various Asiatic tribes forsook the inhospitable taiga and the horrendously bleak tundra and began migrating still further north to the edges of the eternal ice and even beyond. These people moving west populated Greenland, northern Canada and eventually northern Alaska and became known as the Inuit or in more popular parlance, the Eskimo. Another group similar to the Chukchi or the Goldi, island-hopped or maybe just walked from Siberia across what is now known as the Bering Straits into America, and journeying south they became the Red or Amero-Indian people. Oddly the spitz-type dog accompanied the Eskimo people, whereas early explorers found the camps of Amero-Indians crawling with yellow-brown jackal-type dogs which were definitely not of husky type.

The migrating Eskimo bands produced or bred a stocky powerful type of sled or hunting dog, a little wolf-like in appearance, slow in movement, but wonderfully efficient at living on a very frugal diet and at times of hunger becoming food animals themselves, and thus the Greenland husky, now known as the Eskimo dog, came into being.

Ironically, the most constitutionally sound member of the dog world suffered badly from being embraced by the British Kennel Club. Limited numbers of the breed were brought into the country and because of their limited numbers a programme of non too judicious in-breeding became the practice, out of necessity. Sadly, some of the specimens carried the genes of epilepsy – alas, many breeds do – and such is the state of the Eskimo dog in Britain that many breeders have decided not to perpetuate these lines of dog and are now importing specimens from Norway where epilepsy in Eskimo dogs is rare if not unknown.

The Inuit or Eskimo migrations continued across Canada to Alaska and one tribe which settled at Kotzebue Bay became known as the Mahlinuit. This tribe was isolated from other Eskimo communities by distance and cut off from the rest of the world by the somewhat hostile Amero-Indians called the Athabaskans to the south. Inbreeding produced its genetic problems in the dogs, but the same isolation and limited gene banks produced a startling effect on this type of Eskimo dog. Huge powerful brutes weighing up to ten stones began to evolve, some believe aided and abetted by the introduction of the American timber wolf blood though others deny it (and I'm one of these). These huge dogs, the Americans (never a race to master native languages) changed Mahlinuit to Malemute, were the greatest canine powerhorses man has yet produced, one pulled a lorry and truck weighing nearly two tons only a decade ago, and snapped inch thick sisal ropes like a seamstress does a length of cotton, and if unchecked could literally pull a man's arms from the sockets. So powerful are the Malemutes that a special halter has been designed to control them.

Well, so much for the spitz breeds and if the reader is still interested in the Malemute it should be pointed out that while they are reputedly more easily controlled than the other sled dogs, they have the added problem of being God Almighty fighters, capable of settling battles in the bloodiest manner, ferocious enough to please even Jack London. They also have a problem called chondrodysplacia, a disorder caused by a recessive gene which enables a pair of healthy normal Malemutes to be mated together, and to produce hideous little bent-legged dwarf creatures.

To return to my tale, I leaned, almost sacrilegiously on the Dormobile, and listened to this relic of another age enthuse on northern dogs, so different from other breeds that some experts on Eskimo dogs have labelled the type *canis familiaris borealis*. I knew some of the tales, but my ignorance was pathetic besides that of this incredible storyteller who fascinated me, and before I had time to question his wolf dog origin theory or his theory of the population migration, I was launched into a tale wild and woolly enough to excite the heart of Robert W. Service, the Kipling of Canada, let alone an exiled, unhappy, unsuccessful Welsh schoolteacher on his way to God knows where.

Alaska had been the property of Russia at one time. Early explorers had believed that the land was connected to Russia by a land bridge, as indeed at one time it probably was, and Russia coveted and perhaps even valued the land, not only for its timber and extraordinary landscape where river banks were often littered with the tusks and skulls of long-dead mammoths, but primarily because of the huge numbers of seals which populated the islands around the coast. America, however, quick off the mark at realising that the presence of a potentially hostile power on its own doorstep was not advisable, caught the Czar in a moment of financial weakness and bought up Alaska, lock, stock, barrel, seals and timber, for a shade over $7 million in 1867 which was not a moment too soon, for very shortly afterwards tales of the vast mineral wealth of the newly acquired land began to seep out of Alaska.

By the turn of the century the world realised such tales were not exactly exaggerated and that there were literally people digging for gold in the street, though more money was spent extracting the gold than the metal was worth. An amazing variety of people descended on Alaska in the summer of 1897. America has always attracted the most cosmopolitan of settlers but now an ill-equipped band of get-rich-quick prospectors churned up the mud trails twixt Anchorage and Nome in the fabulous Alaskan Gold Rush. Winter, a hard time anywhere north of latitude 60°, dealt harshly with these people, but covered the trails with snow enabling the first of the dog freighters to break through to the gold fields. A variety of sled dogs were used and dogs from setters to German shepherds hauled freight and traveller into the freezing hell of the Yukon and Alaska, sometimes dying like flies when the temperature plummeted to 60° below, or at least some of these southern dogs did and this should be noted. Native dogs, dogs capable of pulling sleds and surviving on a poor inadequate diet in terrifying temperatures, fetched $1000 or more in a country where prices had risen so steeply that even a man working a good claim worked night and day to stay alive let alone prosper. Yet some did prosper and though the lunatic millionaire gamblers beloved by Mark Twain (his tales were based on the more lucrative 1849 Californian gold strike) didn't spring up like mushrooms – there were nevertheless men who had made their fortunes overnight and were willing to lose them, also overnight, by betting on anything and everything. A lawyer with the unlikely name of Albert Fink, was, in addition to being a lawyer, an acute student of human nature and realised that a club to preserve the purity of Arctic sled dogs – there was scarcely a pure bred Eskimo dog in Alaska at this time – would also attract gamblers who had a lively interest in betting on any event from a battle twixt English pit bull dogs and native huskies to dog racing. Attract gamblers, Fink certainly did, but he just about ruined the already questionable lineage of the Alaskan sled dog. Fink's club drew up a race between Nome and a post office in the town of Candle and back – a holy heller of a race some 408 miles long over rock and hill, river and mountain, the only markers of which were the Nome to Candle telegraph line. Straight away the purity of the native breeds came under fire for a Russian fur trader called Goosak, who enjoyed special favours in Siberia, where he had established a company akin to the Hudson Bay Trading Company, had watched the tiny dogs of the Chukchi tribesmen and sensed in them racing potential. Goosak literally dashed across the Bering Straits, bought up a team of Chukchi or Siberian huskies, and came back with his miniature wards, who looked so incongruous alongside the large Alaskan dogs that Robins, a Cockney who ran book on the event, offered odds of 100-1 against the team and 55-1 against the team finishing the race. Goosak was a compulsive gambler and tingled with excitement at the thought of an underdog, and a Russian underdog at that, ripping off the goldfield gamblers and he employed a freighter called Louis Thustrup to race the dogs for him. Sadly, just before the race finished Thustrup became snow-blind and finished third, losing Goosak a fortune and causing him to leave Alaska and seek yet another fortune among the sable-hunting Goldi tribesmen of the Siberian taiga. All in all Goosak seemed to have had a sort of hard-luck-story life and his chequered career as a sable trader ranged from log cabin to White House and sadly back again to log cabin.

However, the racing potential of Goosak's team was seen by a fortune-hunting Scot called Fox Maule Ramsey (his parents must have hated him to give him such a name). Ramsey, a second son of the Earl of Dalhausie, was a typical second son type who was encouraged by his parents to be as wild and profligate as possible – well, with a name like Fox Maule what could you expect? Now, Fox Maule Ramsey knew a bit about Goosak's dealings with the Chukchi and promptly hired a schooner for $2500 and sailed up the Anadyr river collecting dogs from the Chukchi tribesmen at the Siberian settlement of Markova, as bleak and desolate a spot as one could find and one which Czar Nicholas sent discredited army officers to govern. Fox Maule succeeded in buying a somewhat mixed bag of some 70 dogs and sailed home to get badly beaten in the 1909 race but to sweep the board the following year. The time of the destruction of the native Eskimo-type husky was at hand. The following years saw mixed teams of Malemute/foxhound crosses and within five years this mongrel blood had entered the pedigrees of the native dogs thereby totally defeating the Nome Kennel Club founder's goal – serve him right for being called Albert Fink, I suppose.

However, interest in dog racing was dying, although it experienced a temporary revival when a Norwegian freight driver called Leonhard Seppala won against all odds with a team of Siberian huskies in 1915, 1916 and 1917 but the goldfields had played out by this time. Fox Maule Ramsey left Alaska and returned to Scotland to become Earl Dalhausie when his older brother died. Nome became a ghost town, an empty shell of a place, a far cry from the tinsel town of a dozen years before when whore and miner went north to get rich overnight, though judging from the mining records the whores were clear winners every time. The world forgot Alaska and though Jack London kindled an interest in sled dogs in *The Call of the Wild* in 1903, and *White Fang* in 1906, the outside world became involved in a war which seemed a lot more important than teams of dogs racing through unimaginable temperatures. However, in 1925 the self-same war-sated world sat on the edge of its seat while one of the most heroic acts in history took place.

The Eskimos and the Athabaskan Indian had suffered greatly through the gold rush. Abused and ill-treated by the newcomers, often shot dead by way of light relief, they too heaved a sigh of relief when they saw a series of awful winters overwhelm the empty ghost towns and the once churned mud trails become grassed over by the summer tundra plants. Syphilis and other allied diseases still stayed on after the settlers left, and these diseases of 'civilisation' to which the natives had no resistance played havoc with the Alaskans, Eskimo and Athabaskan Indian alike. However, in 1924 an officer of the USA health service called Curtis Welch began to get distressing reports of whole villages being wiped out by a disease called diphtheria, a malaise that scalded and vipered through the Athabaskan Indians and Eskimos, as neither had encountered the disease and hence had no resistance to it. Serum was shipped north from America to Anchorage Alaska, one of the few towns which had survived the vagaries of the gold rush, but here progress ground to a halt. An outsized blizzard had reduced visibility to zero and sent temperatures plummeting to 60° below. The air service at Fairbanks, which in 1925 was primitive anyway, was grounded and the world offered up prayers for the unfortunate, seemingly doomed natives around Nome. However, man is a curious creature and in cases of appalling adversity the most unlikely figures become heroes. A host of dog sled mushers emerged from obscurity, and the press the world over, sensing a truly epic story in the making, gave a life story account of every driver (other than those of Eskimo or Indian descent) involved in bringing the serum the 655 miles relay to Nome. Men like Shannon,

Folger, Nicolai, Seppala and Kasson became world famous overnight as driving through the blinding blizzard and facing enormous dangers they crossed Alaska to deliver the serum. Dog after dog froze on them and blood-stained paw prints marked every foot of the trail, but 5½ days later the package of serum slithered and slid into Nome aboard Kasson's sled. New York Central Park erected a statue to Balto, Kasson's lead dog and the world screamed its applause, and then quite suddenly forgot the dog of the frozen north as some jazz musician pushed the heroic run out of the headlines, and the angular beat of the Charleston drowned the howl of Arctic blizzards and the patter of huskies' feet in the public's fickle interests. A revival took place when Byrd took a band of unfortunate huskies to Antarctica and then inexplicably blew them up after he'd chained them to an iceberg, but the public soon forgot about the atrocity, indeed many were not told of it. Alaska like Siberia became one of those places that everyone knew of by name, but by little else, and interest in sled dogs slumbered and slept.

Interest experienced a revival in the most unlikely way, though certainly not in the most unlikely places. Snowgos, noisy shuffling machines, had made the husky as obsolete as the motor car had made the carthorse, and while Nevada, a long way south, kept interest alive in running winter races with sleds and summer races with rigs of the type sported by my American friend Alaska, Yukon and the North West Territory slumbered and slept through its days of howling gales, punctuated by equally loud howling dogs, the cacophany broken only by the oddly out of place roar of the modern snowgo.

However, when World War II ended abruptly and to use a somewhat sick note somewhat noisily, veterans returning home brought back not only purple hearts, Japanese swords and such like, but also a hint of nostalgia, for nostalgia, a memory of better times perhaps, is one of those sentiments which not only survives but flourishes in times of bloody combat. Veteran Alaskan mushers applauded the ingenuity of the snowgo awhile, admired its technology, its aerodynamic form maybe, even its quiet economy, for it could lie up silent and unfed within dog yards of Huslia, Alakeet and Hughes where a thousand wolf-like curs once howled at every moon and ate their way through an ocean of dried fish each day. Nostalgia is a hard opponent to beat however, and the more you try to smother the life out of her the stronger she gets, and in 1946 the Rendevous Races (spots where fur traders came to sell their wares two hundred years before), began with a prize fit to draw a gasp from a trapper of a matched coat of prime sables, and once more the craze for dog racing began again, and began in earnest. At first the swift-moving Siberian huskies of Seppala featured in the winning teams, but before long crosses with setters, hounds (called targhis hounds) and pointers, began to better them and the whole mixed bunch began to gel – a little slowly perhaps into the relatively pure (and I use the word tongue in cheek for I've seen them) Alaskan huskies, dogs capable of flat-out performances at sixteen miles per hour for a hundred miles a day, and then when someone deemed the breed was good and ready, Joe Remington Sr, who had more than a hint of that damned destructive force called nostalgia, decided to stage the daddy-of-them-all race called the Iditarod, a race following the old serum run, but run by one man and one sorely used team of dogs. It was a race designed to be a nightmare, but the prize of $50 000 for the winner seemed to make a sweet dream out of the most outlandish nightmare. It would be a race of 1169 miles finishing in Nome, Alaska, a race where the physical exertion would make a man's eyebrows crawl with sweat and the sweat form a salty icicle hanging down over his eyes. It would be a race where dogs would be crippled, frozen in the groin and lamed, but a race it was and a monumental one at that – a race so long, so tortuous that it made Phidippides's dash at Marathon seem like a spring jaunt. The craze boomed in the USA.

Here in good old Great Britain things were not the same, but then things are always different in the United Kingdom. The RSPCA, who believe it or not, did a good job of work at one time, and probably still do when not guided by vegan-orientated faceless executives, once had quite a few mindless but pushy members of Parliament under their power, who took a good look at the way draught dogs were used on the roads in Britain and found that their lot was certainly not a happy one and that some were overworked. Thus the British government of that time passed a ban on the dog being used as a draught animal on the public highway, even though a crippled dwarf called Old Lal ran a team of foxhounds as well kept and fed as could be found at the Quorn, up and down the north road putting coach and horse to shame, speed-wise and condition-wise to boot. Society – a nebulous word; it usually means those in power with vested interests, if the word is properly dissected, for English is a versatile language – decided that poor traders who could not afford to buy big draught horses to pull their wares, used large pet mongrels. But the Bishop of Oxford – one who would have certainly disliked yours truly, and had the compliments returned with interest – pointed out that the prohibition of freighting would probably see 20 000, yes, just a mere 20 000, now useless draught dogs hanged – nobody liked dog teams except the folks who owned them. Dogs apparently didn't have souls or feelings – well, not in Oxford anyway. Oxford's eloquence carried the day – after all it was only 20 000 dogs which were to go to the wall anyway – and since 1855 no dog is allowed to draw freight on the highway. Just a few weeks ago a crippled lady whose two pet Alsatians gleefully pulled their mistress to the shops in the wheelchair was fired a warning shot by an RSPCA official, or at least received a visit. No action was taken possibly because the now just a shade out of kilter RSPCA might have found quite a few less coins jingling in their collection boxes – mine for starters. It's a pity really, the society did such a lot of good when it started and should never have been allowed to permit an extremist element to control it, and control it it seems to do.

My American finished his spiel, strapped his rig to his roof rack, proferred his hand, and waved goodbye, while I returned to the van to talk to the now more than petulant Jamie, still quaffing McEwan's.

'Great chap', I uttered.

'I hate 'em.'

'What, dogs, Yanks, rigs, or just about everything?' I queried.

'No,' he said sulkily, 'Atomics', and it was to be two hundred miles before I found out what in the name of God he meant by 'Atomics'.

SOME FACES ROUND THE FIRE

—5—

The Mumpers

I'VE ALWAYS CONSIDERED that Scotland began at Fort William. The English seemed to have nibbled at the southeast region so well that scarcely a 'Mc' can be found, while the Irish invasion of the time shortly after Christ has produced a somewhat different breed of people up as far as Glasgow. However, by Fort William, inns, garages, shops and even the inevitable ice cream vans bear unmistakable hints that Scotland has at least begun there at the end of Loch Ness, a strip of water which almost ripped Scotland in two, geographically speaking, and, culturally speaking just about completed the job. Fort William is as different from Glasgow as Glasgow is from Preston, and judging from the way my Ford Escort van was performing, roughly the same distance as well.

Numerous tracks and country lanes seem to cartwheel into Fort William – enjoy the trees, there are very few twixt Loch Ness and Cape Wrath – and up one of those muddy tracks Jamie, now relatively clear of his alcoholic stupor, urged me to go.

'Worth going, worth going,' he spluttered excitedly, 'bet ye've never seen mumpers', and it now behoves me to explain Jamie's expression.

It's a strange fact that throw a handful, or maybe several handfuls – there seem to be a lot about – of hardened criminals into prison, rapists, murderers, arsonists, paedophiles, and within a month they will have stratified dividing themselves into social layers as clear-cut and distinct as a jam sandwich. Bottom rung (unfortunate choice of phrase perhaps) is the paedophile, the child molester, despised by all, hated, condemned to menial work of the nastiest kind, and the worst places to sleep. Next will come rapists, depending on the nature of the rape and the age of the victim. Arsonists are treated as untouchables beyond any social pale, too crazy to deserve a niche in the criminal structure, while murderers regardless of the ferocities of their crimes and the horror of the acts they have perpetrated will invariably occupy top rung of this rather run-down micro-society. Man is like that, I suppose, obsessed with a desire to stratify, to make social systems. For Pete's sake, don't knock the Hindus with their Brahmins and structures descending to their untouchables. They simply have the system down to a fine workable art, while the rest of us play at stratification, invariably making a mess of it until drawing room 'Reds' (a bit like energetic editions of Dad, but confined to the middle class), invariably trigger off a horrendous civil war which, when the dust of battle has settled, finds mankind making what he considers to be a better new world but a world with just the same jam sandwich class structure as before, just as class-orientated, just as messy, and just as spiteful. OK. sociology/political lesson over and now back to the mumpers.

Nowhere outside of the strictest Hindu sects is the class system more rigid, less relenting, and subject to such little change as amongst the people of the drom – the travelling folk. Somehow or other such castes are entirely related to certain taboos, the violations of which determine the caste to which individuals belong. Long before the bleak autumnal night ahead of us was finished, my education regarding the caste structure of the dromengro would have been well and truly enlarged and I would have been treated to a very depressing glimpse of the caste which correspond to the least touchable of the untouchables amongst the more primitive Hindu sects.

However, to return to the caste structure which prevails amongst those who seek to travel the roads, rather than dwell in settled places – the dromengro and the kerengro, terms which are a lingua franca amongst travelling folk be they Romany-blooded or not. Top of this strange and on first impression outlandish system, for all itinerants look alike to those who know nothing of them, are the pure bred or nearly pure bred Romanies, families which are not only well known and well-respected by fellow dromengros but also held in some esteem by the gorgios (outsiders) who have had dealings with them. Families like the Lees, and the Boswells of fortune-telling fame (Urania Boswell predicted the time and nature of her own death so Brian Vesey Fitz-gerald once assured me) are trusted and treated with great respect by the travellers of the Midlands where many have chosen to settle though others still travel; the women selling pegs and curious, stick-made dyed gypsy flowers; and the men tarmacadaming roads, shoeing recalcitrant horses and repairing curious outlandish (and outmoded) farm imple-ments, a prosperous trade indeed for any skilled metal worker, now that the 'back to the earth cult' has started up once again.

Families like the Ingrams are held in similar high regard in North

Wales, a taciturn, rather shy type of Romany who in addition to being able to perform the customary gypsy crafts, were also famed for their skills at the fast-dying art of harping. Queen Victoria's harper was an Ingram, a man who spoke not only English and the nasal north Welsh dialect, but also when surrounded by others of similar breeding to his own, the deep pure Romany once spoken in the Bala area where Sampson, the great student of itinerant languages, spent some time to compile his dictionary of Romany.

Most of the high caste clans are fastidiously clean, observing strict taboos about cleanliness and the definition of work between men and women, and their caravans are bedecked with fortunes in the form of Crown Derby and expensive crockery beyond the price of the average house dweller. I once had tea with George Gaskin, the caravan maker who offered me tea in a cup worth £450. I shuddered and delicately refused the cup, settling for a Woolworth's 25p mug instead. He took no offence but simply shrugged his shoulders at my reluctance to partake of what he considered to be the finer things of life.

Next down the social strata of the dromengo – pure bred Romanies consider the chasm twixt these people and themselves very great indeed – are the half bred Romanies or 'posh rats' (posh – half, rat – blood), although now that the social structure of the upper echelon is breaking up a little, such terms as 'posh rats' are seldom met, for the majority of Romany families have a little outsider, or quite a lot of outsider, blood in their veins.

A hundred years ago so strict was the rule regarding purity of clan and checking of pedigree for fear of incest or bringing in undesirable qualities, that it was once said that a Lee only married a Lee. A month ago an itinerant band was forced to come to a local school, and while the child was called Lee after his father, his mother retained her maiden name of Rylatt. A century ago a relationship between a Romany and a gorgio was frowned on and the couple and their children ostracised. Now the schism between the two castes is slowly breaking down.

Not so the differences between the Romanies, posh rats and the didikais, groups of people who still adhere to a travelling way of life but have a quarter or even less than a quarter Romany blood in their veins. Didikais are practically undetectable as being anything other than pure bred Romanies by outsiders, but those with a knowledge of the people of the roads see differences quickly and clearly. The food, the hygiene, the sexual taboos which govern the life of the pure Romany, and to a certain extent the posh rat, are either absent or diluted in the didikais. A few years ago a Romany by the name of Mo Smith and I went seeking a vardo stove amongst a camp of very tidy-looking didikais, who politely offered us tea. I accepted, Mo declined. Later he explained that he had seen them wash out clothes in the same bowl they had used to wash the cups. For this reason he will refuse tea at my house unless he rinses out the cup before he pours his own tea. Such curious taboos, called 'Maremais' amongst itinerants, are strictly observed by the upper castes but are often neglected by many didikais.

There is almost a contempt of the didikai amongst the Romanies, and many a Romany will move site if a didikai family moves on to his pitch; others deny any relationship with didikai families even though the families bear the same typical Romany surnames. It is here the division of the castes exists, not twixt the Romany and the posh rat as most gypsiologists believe, for the majority of Romanies believe that if a posh rat does not marry back into his own people, he usually acquires a wife who is somewhat less than socially desirable and is an outcast amongst gorgios as well as amongst travellers.

Ranking level with the didikai in the hierarchy of the road are the mixed, varied and colourful group known as tinkers in England, and tinklers in Scotland, which share as a common denominator a certain wildness of character outside the realms of true Romany behaviour. The chances are these people, who spoke a bastard Irish tongue called 'Shelta', and a sort of secret almost Freemasonic language called Bealagair Na Saer, were a tribe or clan considerably older than the gypsy or Romany bands and so similar to the ways of the gypsies – they mended pots and pans, acted as amateur veterinary surgeons – that they may well have been descendants of Indo-European Criminal tribe migrants moving west and pre-dating the modern Romany movements by 2000 years. Culain, the smith of the legend of Cuhulain had strange enough habits to make him a shade different from the rest of the clans, and his skill in working iron goods makes him once again suspect. However, unlike the Romany peoples the taboos are almost totally absent, and the laws that govern the clans are as often as not decided there and then by fist and foot as by any ancient tribal custom.

When they came to Britain heaven only knows. Perhaps they arrived as armourers with the invading Scots who were an Irish tribe (if you can skip back a few confusing pages), just as many gypsiologists believe that many of the gypsies of Europe arrived with the hordes of Ghengis Khan, acting as artificers to his army. However, and one can damn every last corn-growing Englishman, the majority of the wretched Irish were driven here by the misery brought about by the Irish Potato Famine (1839–1842) when the wheat fields of Canada had produced such a surplus as to be able to feed the world and cheaply at that, but English Corn Laws prohibited its import – a bitter time – one best forgotten or perhaps one which should be well remembered. Hundreds of Irish sold every stick of furniture, every patch of land for a passage to

England, and sought work anywhere in the worst areas of the cities where the language of Shelta eased and slithered into thieves cant, or travelled along the Welsh and Scots borders. Their encounters with the Romanies were short, bloody and grossly over-glamorised in gypsy folklore. Despite the fact that the Romany was producing more than its share of bare-knuckle champions in the grim fist-breaking days before the Marquis of Queensberry's time, The Romany of the Welsh Marches came upon a ferocious Fi-Fo-Fum type battler, born out of savage and desperate poverty, rather than conceived out of guile and ability to suss out a 'mark'. The tales of their encounters in the 1850s–1870s are still beloved by those whose interests are in gypsy lore, but those same tales are lamentably wrong. The Irish tinker cast in solid brainless brawn, hurt so often by indignity, the brutality of anti-Irish laws, was a juggernaut of flesh impossible to stop until he was killed and the stock that spawned the Anglo-Welsh March Irish tinker and the Highland tinkler, also produced John L. Sullivan, the Boston Strong Boy. The gypsy faired badly against these newcomers, and took to different routes, hoping that the inclement elements and the inclement peasantry (for the land around Offas' Dyke has known penury enough not to be known for its generosity), would deal with the bands of newcomers. Some settled and thieved, others as gifted at music as the Romanies, became itinerant musicians.

Tony Capstick of Sheffield Radio and Channel Four tells a fabulous tale of the typical tinker band. Thurso was the scene of a folk festival and Capstick – a gentle and lovable man – was thirty on one Saturday night of the festival, feeling far from Mexborough and further still from wife and family. The Irish tinkers, self-taught musicians, as talented as they were tough, heard of Capstick's calamity. They played hell in Thurso, knocking up every baker in that quiet fishing town, and at breakfast in the boarding house where the group stayed, presented Capstick with a huge birthday cake. A strange mix are the Irish tinker with their bell-like brogue and half-mad ways – a strange and curious folk indeed.

Of the last of the social hierarchy, the dregs of the vat of human ale, the lees and assorted pieces which reside in the fermenting barrel of life, there is little to say that is happy, joyful, complimentary or, sadness of sadness, even hopeful, for whereas the people of the road are regarded as the outcasts of society, the pariahs, whom every household is quick to phone the 'authorities' to move them on, the dromengro – the people of the road – too have their pariahs, though perhaps they are apt to be a little more kindly to the folk who live the ways of the mumpers.

Mumpers seldom, if ever, come from Romany or Romany/tinker families, though the whole spectrum of life seems to be present at some camps at some time or other. The bearded, heavy-booted tramp, clothes patched, hair unattacked by barbers could be classified as a mumper, a man of no fixed abode, a man with no obvious family connections, nor indeed any fixed means of support, but the majority of the group who are collectively known as 'mumpers' are a far cry from the hale and hearty tramps of the W. H. Davies autobiography or the husky Jack London bum edging his way through a once pollution-free California without a trouble in the world, not giving a damn for anyone or anything. As a whole mumpers are the most pitiable of people, the ultimate dropouts of the human race, as indeed I suppose I am a dropout in my own quiet eccentric way. Forget the carefree tramp, rucksack on back, striding along the country lanes, the envy of every worried potential coronary victim, Pierre Cardin clad executive passing him in his gleaming new BMW. The typical mumper has nothing to envy and the freedom and pride so brazenly manifested by the heavy-booted tramp has long been corroded, eroded and subdued in a mumper who has spent a mere two years on the road. Seemingly, so my sparse research into this wretched detritus of humanity has led me to believe, it takes two years to make a person into a qualified and irretrievable mumper. The first year may be hard and tough, the summers wet, the spring dull, the autumn muddy and reeking of decay, and the winter a frozen hell, but man somehow has that strange often inexplicable hope that things will turn out for the better, and believes that nothing he can experience will be as bad as the year through which he has lived. The next year usually turns out to be just a shade worse, and dispirited, health broken, arthritis (the curse of all mumpers) setting in, the mumper becomes a fully fledged member of the fraternity, low in spirit, pride evaporated like dew in the morning, and wanting nor expecting nothing of tomorrow. It's a hurry-on-down world and at the end of the ride is the inevitable 'death from exposure' coroner's verdict if the mumper is lucky, or if not so lucky to be found in the nick of time by some social worker and brought back to the sane, antiseptic world that the mumper has sought to forget, and into which he or she can now never fit. Like damaged captive sparrows taken in by kindly old ladies on sub-zero nights, fed on surfeits of Christmas cake, they look towards the great outdoors and freedom, but their bodies, wracked and worn by hard labour and poor food, their joints swollen with arthritis, will prevent their fluttering attempts to freedom, and within a year they will waste away to nothing, finally expiring in some sterile ward, defying a head-scratching coroner to pass a verdict on the manner of their demise. From day one there is no hope for the mumper. Tramps often come off the road to write successful novels or poetry, but the lot of the mumper is written in the sand and when the wind blows, the words, and the mumper with them, are forgotten.

I must confess I had seen mumpers and had no wish to witness another pitiable band, but goaded by Jamie's excited voice and his arm-waving directions, I turned the van off the road and headed down a bumpy muddy path, the mud made fibrous by the leaves which bestrewed the track. Harvested and now ploughed fields above us gave an air of desolation to the scene, an aura of a cold and cheerless time in a man's life, rather than a seasonal scene from a Constable painting. At the end of the track was an old and very tattered guards' wagon, decaying rapidly despite its pickled creosote woodwork, and various cracks, missing boards and holes had been stuffed with heather, bracken and a variety of clothes, which were obviously too rotted to be worn.

Even as I pulled up alongside the van, the stench from the inside of the wagon struck me full in the face – the sort of smell one associates with the kitchen of an overburdened slattern who has heard of neither hygiene nor birth control. Yet even through this miasma and urinous stink, a far more ominous odour seemed to be present, an odour I couldn't place at the time, but now as I write, shortly after my release from an intensive care ward, I know only too well.

I glanced across at Jamie and noticed a faint sneering smile lighten his lips. I had tolerated his vile habits, been amused by his curiously antisocial ways, laughed out loud at his barbarous humour, but now as I watched his amused face as he viewed this pitiful human menagerie, saw his superior attitude manifest itself, heard him snigger at these pitiable wretches, I felt a sudden dislike for him, a dislike I had to restrain lest it should grow to a hatred that would have caused me to pound his head repeatedly against the windscreen, until no smile, sneer or face for that matter remained on that inane and brutal head. I gripped the steering wheel until the sensation passed and the awful desire to hurt Jamie subsided, but when I glanced across at him he was still smirking at the plight of the unfortunates.

Six people made up Jamie's mumper band, five of them ragged emaciated pathetic wretches reached straight out of a Ken Russell film. I was an intruder, a sightseer, not a visitor, and for one moment I was struck with a curious notion as to whether sadistic German officers ever took civilian personnel for a day out to watch the more wretched or dispirited camp inmates at Treblinka. I felt ashamed that Jamie had cajoled, coaxed, pressed me into an evening's entertainment to watch these unfortunates. Three males, and three females made up the group, and I contemptuously ignored Jamie's question as to which couples I considered were paired up – though Romanies regard mumpers as the most promiscuous of people, breeding like rabbits, producing a superfluity of children, most of whom die of neglect shortly after childbirth.

This band however seemed more concerned with living out the day in that fast-chilling Scottish autumn evening, than indulging in some Bacchic orgy in that evil-smelling railway truck. Each day lived must have represented a triumph for these pathetic people, each evening, each bedding down to sleep, the last round of a gruelling fifteen-round contest.

They all seemed to have known Jamie and the majority treated him cordially despite his nudges in my ribs and the sneering grin that spread over his Asiatic face, as each one of the unfortunates appeared.

'Come sit around the yog' (a term for a fire used by Chalo and Kalderashi gypsies and Irish tinkers alike). 'Jamie, come sit here,' an elderly hag patted a worn tree stump which was used as a stool.

The evening was darkening quickly as autumnal evenings in that part of Scotland are wont to do, and a flash of firelight outlined the speaker, making her resemble one of the witches from Macbeth, overdone by the make-up artist at the RSC. The speaker was a scrawny figure whose gesture of friendship included a smile which indicated that the majority of her teeth were missing, and the remaining incisor teeth – always the last to disintegrate – were blackened with decay and misuse. She put her arm around Jamie, who edged rather than shrank away.

'I've known Jamie since he were a bairn. His gran lived in the caves at Staxigoe [a village near Wick]. It were right nice in them caves, she kept them real clean.'

'Lying bastard,' muttered Jamie, a flash of embarrassment suffusing his Asiatic face.

I watched him, my head tilted to one side, a curious and irritating habit I have, for the tale, however incongruous, had a ring of truth about it. A band of tinkers had settled in a cave somewhere in Scotland, only to be evicted by an abnormally high tide and the old lady's tale had more than just a ring of truth about it.

'She's been on the bleeding meths again, I bet,' he whispered, just loud enough for the old lady to hear, but she ignored his insult as the coming of the dusk heralded the more important preparation of the evening meal.

The band went about their respective tasks, preparing a sort of stew in a large pea or bean tin, the sort normally purchased by cafés and capable of holding close on a gallon of food. A length of sheep 'tension' wire was attached to the tin to act as a handle and the women of the group busied themselves by scraping carrots, potatoes, onions and sheep turnips with almost meticulous care, despite their filthy, dirt-ingrained hands. One man, a villainous-looking brute whose face never boasted a smile, took out an ugly, broken-bladed Bowie knife and with an odd almost unwholesome glee began to slash into a corned beef tin, gouging its contents into the broth which was beginning to boil within the sheep wire-handled pea tin cooking pot. He took a savage stab at the base of the corn beef can, a grimace twisting his thin lips, and hurled the can backwards inside the railway truck.

The light and heat of the fire and the scent of the cooking vegetables had brought the band near to the fire, and a tall, well-built man of about forty, a man who still managed to maintain a hint of dignity despite his patched clothes, stoked up the flames with a pile of dead whin (gorse) until the spark-exploding flames illuminated the contents of the railway carriage. The most hardened of sadists, the most callous of men, would have been reduced to pity by the sight within the carriage, and even Jamie's perpetual and annoying snigger died in his throat. He nudged me slyly to provoke a response and I jabbed him with my elbow bringing a hiss of pain from him.

The conflict was broken suddenly by Annie, the blackened-toothed, hag-like figure, who sensing Fathom and Penguin sniffing around her smoke and sweat-smelling hair said, 'Ain't your dogs lovely, Mister? I 'ad a dog once, a little white one, I fink it was called a Malteser.'

'I think you mean a Maltese,' said the quiet, cultured voice of the man who was stoking up the fire with dead whin. I glanced around and saw that, despite the fact that the man's face was heavily bearded, he looked totally out of place in a setting which resembled the 'court of the deformed' in one of Sergeane Colon's novels. I stared at him perhaps a little too long I think, and he slunk into the shadows to refurbish the fire.

'If dem dogs come near me, I'll stab 'em with this knife,' came an angry shout from a man, maybe in his late fifties, who seconds ago had eviscerated a corn beef tin with the same weapon.

'That's Bomber,' hissed Jamie with more than a hint of respect or perhaps more aptly fear.

The villainous-looking brute wore a bomber jacket, the leather of which had long parted company with the underneath fabric.

'They do say', said Jamie almost reverently, 'he took that jacket offen a man he killed.'

'I'll slash 'em, cut 'em to pieces if they come near me,' Bomber raged at Penguin and Fathom.

'There's no need for that, Bomber,' said the quiet dignified voice, and Bomber went back again dragging an old railway sleeper into the fire to take out his vengeance on it.

'I hate dogs, specially them that sniff,' he uttered in a rather subdued manner as if afraid of the quiet dignified figure who kept building up the fire. 'Specially those that sniff,' he repeated giving the railway sleeper a particularly savage blow.

I've taught boys of Bomber's ilk for years, boys who reacted wildly and insanely to each and every insult, real or imaginary, and I knew Fathom and Penguin's natural sychophantic tendencies and predisposition for plate-licking placed them in deadly peril. I stood up to put them back in the van only to find Bomber leap up, thrusting the blade through the flames at me.

'Just touch me, go on, just try,' roared the tormented soul, 'just you try.'

I froze immediately. I've taught psychopaths for years, and know that under such circumstances no action is the best action. I glanced up and saw Bomber's face twist into an animal-like snarl, a snarl which in a wild beast could have been a prelude to an attack.

'He's just putting the dogs away, not to offend you, Bomber,' said a quiet, soothing voice.

Bomber sank down to a crouch hacking furiously at the log, muttering, 'Just try, go on, just try.'

I felt a cold chill down my back and the driest of tastes in my mouth as I shepherded the dogs into the van.

'Pity,' said Annie, scratching herself in a place where no lady should, 'I likes dogs. They could have licked my plate.' ('Probably died,' hissed Jamie.)

My concentration was once again broken by a cry of 'Watch out, there's a pile of dry whin about to come on', and the flames shot higher than before, revealing the contents of the railway van – five urinous, stained mattresses, recovered like as not from the local rubbish dump, each mattress covered with a liana-like growth of rags. I sensed a movement under one of the piles of rags.

'Come on Megan love. Food is almost up,' cajoled Annie.

A pale, paper-thin-skinned woman of an indefinable age ambled across to the fire and sat down as if almost in a trance.

The firelight illuminated her face, the skin drawn tightly across the cheek bones, the hair a filthy mess of unkempt dirt, made yellow by constant contact with wet wood smoke, smelling slightly of stale vomit with a hint of something necrotic and even more unpleasant. The sculptor Rodin had once carved a statue, a masterpiece in hidden meaning, a little like one of those puzzles, where numerous faces are hidden amongst foliage and rocks, and he had called it his masterpiece, 'The Once Beautiful Heaulmiere' – a model of a very much 'gone to seed' courtesan who had been abused by kings and dukes, princes and earls, and passed down the line until she resided amongst the most pitiable creatures of the Paris gutters. Rodin had carved a ravaged old woman, or what appeared as a ravaged old woman, until one looked carefully at the statue, and saw highlights of what must have been a raging beauty of the sort men turned around to watch. What emerged from the filthy van was a flesh and blood – though God knows there was little enough flesh, and possibly less blood – version of the statue, a pitiful degenerate travesty of what must once have been a lovely woman.

'Penny for your thoughts?' said the tender of the fire who had been studying my face a little more than casually.

'Villon,' I replied quietly, thinking that the fire-minder wouldn't have an idea of what I meant, for Villon's poem had been the subject of Rodin's statue.

He smiled and came out with the appropriate quote about the courtesan in immaculate medieval French and my head shot up in amazement.

'For most of us the world has had a bad-to-worse-to-worst note about it,' he replied, and once more disappeared into the darkness to fetch another bundle of dried furze.

Annie began serving out the food using a home-made scoop made from some baby food soup tin, attached to sheep wire, and dishing out on to enamel plates where precious little of the steel was protected by the enamelling.

'Not too much for me,' the quiet, bearded man who had returned once more murmured. 'Remember my condition,' he touched his side below his left rib indicating he suffered from a hiatus hernia.

'I'll eat 'is,' said Jimmy, a diminutive Glaswegian of maybe fifty who still looked moderately clean and tidy amidst a scene of squalor to put a Third World poster to shame.

'S'mine,' snarled Bomber, snatching the plate spilling much of the contents, though it was apparent from the start that the possession of the plate was more important than the contents to this disturbed troll-like beast. Jimmy bristled like a dog preparing to attack, but fearing the outcome of the encounter, and the pair stared at each other as if willing to do battle to the death for a dish of ill-cooked hash. I watched in wonder, suddenly reflecting on how I'd watched two public school lads fight over a matter equally pointless, a matter they considered 'the principle of the thing'. Jimmy and the half-mad Bomber continued to stare like two low-grade mammals set up as an experiment for Lorenz to observe.

'Give it back, Bomber,' said an effete soothing voice and added slightly more harshly, 'Now!' and Bomber with a curse ingraciously passed back the now half-empty plate to Jimmy and set about the railway sleeper with his Bowie knife once more, attacking it with even greater ferocity.

The action caused what can only be described as an atmosphere, a bad feeling and the band ate their meal in silence, using spoons and pieces of bread as their only cutlery. Annie scooped into the pan and offered both Jamie and me a plateful which we both declined, perhaps a little ungraciously. The meal hastily over, the band sat back as the fire blazed brightly, now that the dried whin had caused the railway sleeper, still hacked by Bomber, to catch alight.

My insatiable curiosity which has on numerous occasions damn nigh been the death of me, once again got the better of me. Gypsies and tinkers are usually reluctant to tell tales of their own lives and the tales which are told are invariably lies made up to please a paying audience or to sell some useless item of which they wish to dispose. The result is of course that most gypsiologists finish up writing books and scientific papers which would cause the most naive Romany child to explode with laughter. The band of mumpers seemed more forthcoming, more like the traveller who befriended the fugitive Toad in *Wind in the Willows*, and I decided to chance my luck stupidly and gauchely as usual, for I am gifted with neither tact nor charm. I toyed with a way in, a way which wouldn't hurt too much, a way of finding out what common bond had cemented these poor wretches together, but as I have said I have never been gifted with tact.

'What has brought you all to this?' I blurted out.

I had stopped short of 'state of penury, wretchedness, filth, *etc*?' but the silence I provoked left me in no doubt that they knew what I was hinting at, and I felt like biting off my tongue. One minute I had been the centre of their somewhat limited hospitality and now I was a stranger quizzing, prying, nosing around into what had made them outcasts from society, reject items on the production belt of life. Jimmy simply stared hard into the fire, the eloquent fire-furbisher became silent, Bomber hacked even harder at the burning railway sleeper, muttering oaths and curses at no one in particular and all in general. Megan, the emaciated transparent-skinned woman, simply rocked on her heels a little harder than she had a second or so before, and the near imbecile girl next to her giggled even more inanely, though I doubted if she understood the question. I felt a sort of bristling enmity towards me and I knew they were justly hurt. I had intruded on their private world, been offered friendship and hospitality, and it was I, not they, who had violated the codes of good behaviour and civility. It took seconds to break the hostile silence.

Annie spoke first.

'All of us, 'cepting Jimmy, is up here tatty-picking, but I 'spect you means why is we all mumpers, like?'

I felt too embarrassed to answer or even to nod. Annie sensed my predicament and literally came to my rescue.

'Don't worry, love. None of us' – she cast a somewhat doubtful glance at Bomber though – 'is upset that you've asked.'

The inane, near-idiot girl whom I later discovered was called Katie giggled imbecilicly, showing a set of incredibly short piranha-like teeth. She was an ageless person, who could have been any age between 20 and 40, the sort of person life seems to avoid aging, the sort of person who is mercifully untouched by this very unkind world.

'I'll tell you how I got to be a mumper if you like,' said Annie shuffling her ragged clothes about her.

She began her tale unashamedly, as she was seemingly unashamed by her filthy, ill-fitting clothes, her dirt-ingrained hands, and her lank and matted hair, and as she shuffled to a comfortable position to tell her tale, a stench of stale faeces one finds in the houses of the senile wafted towards me, filling me with a feeling of nausea and causing Jamie to (rudely) peg his nose.

I was astonished to find she was a month younger than I was, if she told the truth, but whereas time had been kind to the feeble-minded Katie it had wrought havoc on Annie, and a casual observer might have guessed her age at sixty or even a shade more. Annie had been born near Sheffield. Her father hadn't deemed it good policy to marry her mother and had left the district shortly after Annie's conception. Her mother had been the mistress of maybe a score of American servicemen, everyone probably using her to the full, some treating her kindly perhaps, others a little less so before moving on. Annie must have known half a century of uncles before the war ended, and the public, no longer needing American aid, had promptly labelled her mother as a 'tart'. Annie caught the shunting effect, the animosity God-fearing people had shown her mother, a confused eneuretic, unable to control the contents of either her bowels or bladder, she became the reason why her mother considered she was unable to keep a regular beau, and Annie became a chopping block on which her mother could vent her spleen when yet another boyfriend rejected her. One day Annie had returned from school with a minor reading prize, probably her one and only academic success in a world which was destined to be forever hostile to her, only to find her mother had left home; 'flitted', Annie had called the action, a curious expression though perhaps one which needs no explanation.

A dozen foster homes had followed in the wake of the departing mother, each home passing the wretched child to another, for Annie had never become house-trained so to speak. When she became fifteen she tried various jobs, but no employer, not even the most kindly Dickensian-type philanthropist, kept on workers with Annie's problems, and slowly but surely Annie edged towards an itinerant way of life, living where she was tolerated, staying for as long as her fellow itinerants could endure her unfortunate habits.

She had hop-picked in Kent, fruit-picked in Worcester, and was now wintering north again, hopeful that the bumper potato crop the pleasant summer had bred would provide a few weeks work for hands which were already misshapen from arthritis, and a back which was already developing a very serious form of sciatica. I looked down at her feet for no particular reason I could think of, and noted she was wearing one man's shoe and one high-heeled woman's shoe with a peek-a-boo toe, and this footwear was probably the cause of the hideous limp I had noticed when I first met Annie. Her tale became meaningless, filled with silly comments, a morass of pointless reflections on a life filled with misery, drudgery and rejection.

'D'you know I was picked up for street-walking in Liverpool,' she reflected a moment, 'or was it Manchester,' she said indignantly. 'Me, for street-walking, and no man has even so much as touched me. Never, I can tell you,' she went on with an almost fierce pride at her thoroughly undesirable virginity.

I closed my eyes and saw not the evil-smelling Annie, but Bessie Bighead straight out of Milkwood, unloved, unwanted and unlovely, and felt a sudden feeling akin to hatred for the police officer who had arrested this wretched and obviously undesirable creature wondering what nasty streak lurked in this man's inner soul that he considered it necessary for the public good to bring in this odd creature for questioning, a pitiful travesty of a woman, whom no man would find desirable. What embarrasing interrogation had Annie undergone? What entertainment had she provided the night shift, before they had allowed her to limp out in her odd footwear? I felt a bitter resentment against a police force who would employ a sadist of the type who would gleefully arrest this pitiable down and out, and I became ashamed that I had been working in what is known as a deprived area and worked hand in hand with the police. Had I assisted fiends who obtained similar kicks by arresting and interrogating those equally unfortunate? Annie could not have been totally unaware that the world sniggered up its sleeve at her odd appearance and held its nose as she passed, and I wondered if the interrogation of this wretch in the cold, antiseptic interview room, which would have intensified Annie's stench, had further damaged an already brutally mutilated soul. My respect for our police force took a nosedive at that point in my life.

'This is a photograph of my Mum,' Annie said, proffering a faded and grubby snapshot of a tarty-looking blonde woman, sporting an Andrew Sisters type hairstyle. Annie smiled as she gazed at the snapshot, crooning over the photograph of the woman who had reduced

Annie to the life she was now leading. 'She were right lovely, my Mum,' she said nostalgically.

'It is indeed a strange person who can find no one to love', said a man called Confucius, and Annie clung on to this photograph as her dearest possession. I closed my eyes and rocked on my heels as did the demented Megan, and saw an elderly tarty woman living with some nondescript man in an equally nondescript council estate, and wondered if she ever thought what had become of her eneuretic daughter.

Bomber continued to hack at the now rapidly burning railway sleeper. It would be difficult to like a person of his ilk and only a mother could have loved him. He added nothing to the conversation and only when something Annie said made him drive the blade deeper into the log, did I realise that he was listening to the chatter going on around him. He had lived as he pleased, so Annie intimated in a fearful whisper, perhaps making enemies amongst gorgios and travellers alike. The rest of the group apart from the silent, soft-spoken sage-like man and the distant and near catatonic Megan, feared his vicious and capricious temper, his tendency to irrational fury and his quickness to take offence. Bomber, the Arabs would say, had his destiny written in the sand for it was inevitable what would happen to him. He already disliked most of humanity and was working on learning how to dislike the rest. Sooner or later one of his insane temper bouts would lead him to kill a man or perhaps, if he met a man whose disposition was more evil and venomous than his own, he would be the one to be killed. Despised and rejected, he would undoubtedly also have been acquainted with grief if people of Bomber's ilk ever really got to know the genuine meaning of the word grief. Seemingly he'd been married once – Annie had whispered that he used to knock his wife about 'summat dreadful' until she left him, hiding away lest he should find her. A man like Bomber is a social pariah from birth, with the seeds of destruction already planted in him. In a primitive society, he would have met with some primitive propitious ritual death years ago. Now approaching sixty he was becoming more hateful and more hated by the day. Curiously, he fascinated me in the way a dangerous unpredictable animal fascinates me, and I could not but wonder what accident or freak of nature had brought about this wild desire to hurt or to rend asunder anything near to him. Had society ill-treated him at a formitive age in his youth? Maybe fate, ever the cruel jester, had played some unpleasant trick on him, causing all to hate him. As I watched his wild-eyed face, his unkempt beard, as his hacking action on the log caused a flame to illuminate his face, I saw him as Barabas the Robber, pardoned by the mob while another ascended the cross to take his place, but unlike Barabas, when Bomber met his destiny there would be no one to plead his case or ask for clemency. He stared hard at the sleeper a moment or so and then went to work with the knife with an almost frenzied action, muttering something inaudible as he did so.

I've taught a dozen or so boys with Bomber's disposition, people who have declared war against society as a whole, boys who eventually kill or are killed as a result of an attack on someone who has inadvertently set off some fuse in their mechanism, but Bomber, Bomber with his steel knife, hacking slivers of wood from the sleeper, glancing up at me from time to time, his eyes made wilder by the blazing branches of the furze, caused a cold shivery tingle to run up my spine and I freely confess I was afraid of him. Procrustes, Sinon and Fe Fi Fo Fum are not demons formed from the fabric of human dreams, they are merely descriptions of people that early man, legend-creating man, had met in his wanderings, and Bomber too had he lived maybe a thousand or so years ago might have been woven into some ugly tale of trolls, demons and flesh-eating fiends. I tried not to look at him, not to stare, despite my fascination with him, lest my interest might upset him and drive him to a bout of frenzy.

Jimmy, a medium-sized pink-faced man, was neat, clean shaven and tidy and his check shirt showed evidence of only a few days' dirt. During the summer times he worked as a sort of general 'go for' in transport cafés, washing up and cleaning toilets in exchange for food and board. The owners of such establishments were careful not to pay him in coin, for if given money he drank and ran amock, becoming insanely drunk on a minute quantity of liquor, taking offence at everything and anything he saw, and believing that any conversation he overheard was something whispered about him. Sober, he was pleasant and sociable, meticulously clean in his habits. Drunk, he became viciously paranoid, out to avenge any insult, real or imaginary. The tatty-picking wasn't for him, for he complained of a bad back, the perennial complaint of the malingerer, and his hands were soft and pink as a result of constant contact with washing-up liquid. Earlier that summer he had worked in a Midlands transport café, as usual exchanging his labour for board and lodge, until one night by a stroke of luck (good or ill, one might question) had found a fiver and drank the lot, becoming raving, helplessly drunk and wickedly vicious. A deaf mute, a lad of maybe twenty and a frequent visitor to the café, had irritated Jimmy by his wild gestures and gesticulations he used to communicate with the speaking public, and Jimmy, convinced the poor devil was poking fun at him, had attacked him with a fork, wounding him slightly. Jimmy had received a spell of psychiatric treatment for his crime, together with a set of new clothes and a general tidy up. ('I don't go to places like nut houses or hostels mysel,' confided Annie, 'they delouse you, make you bath all naked, and if'n you wets yer bed they make you change it in front of all the others watching.') The weather was colder now and the rest of the mumpers would set out to lift the tatties, but Jimmy would willingly suffer the indignity of yet another delousing and a medical examination in some hostel or other to sit out the worst of the winter meekly obeying its rules, observing its often curious, humiliating and pointless rituals until the spring came and he would set off into the Midlands to try to earn his keep at one of the few cafés which still tolerated him. I drifted into reverie, reflecting on how pointless and meaningless such a life must be, feeling perhaps a little smug, a little 'holier than thou' until I was jolted back to reality by the fact that my own life was just as meaningless, just as repetitious and a damned sight less free than Jimmy's. My nine-to-four day was simply a microcosmic replica of his year, and the chances are that he had a hell of a sight more out of life than I was having. I glanced up, caught his eye, both of us looking away while once again he cleared his throat and spat noisily into the fire.

Katie, poor imbecilic Katie, who was maybe twenty-three but could have been much older, chattered inanely and incessantly without needing a reply. She somehow seemed like an appendage of the rapidly aging Annie, enjoying some protection or affection from the pitiful odd-shoed piece of human jetsam, relying on Annie, perhaps as a prop, just as did the feeble-minded giant Lennie relied on George in Steinbeck's *Of Mice and Men.* That summer both had spent their time fruit-picking in the Midlands, but Katie simple-minded and silly couldn't meet the daily quota required by the owner of the farm, despite the fact that Annie had helped fill her punnets. Katie ate more than she picked, and her mouth was a permanent mess of strawberry juice until the day she was sacked. With the hard graft of the potato harvest and no job is more back-breaking or soul-destroying – Katie almost certainly wouldn't be up to it unless the arthritic Annie could do her own share of the labour and a bit more besides. Katie would invariably be told, yet once more, that 'she wasn't up to the job'. Strangely the cares of the world had failed to age Katie and she looked incredibly juvenile, possibly with an IQ well below 70 and, as I gazed across the fire and watched her giggling, and her laughter at pointless and unfunny comments, I thought back to the days when I was forced to spend a week 'observing' at a school for the educationally sub-normal, a place which rang with happy laughter from adolescents, blissfully unaware of the hostile world which awaited them outside the sheltering walls of the school. Were the teachers morally correct in teaching such children that the world would accept them as equals, despite their simple ways and slow and seemingly silly behaviour? Katie had run away from home at sixteen, so Annie informed us because her father had taken an unwholesome interest in her. I felt Jamie stiffen. The tales of 'Hurry on Down' misery we had heard had not bothered him at all, but the thought of a father forcing his attentions on a backward child had jarred him somewhat.

'Bastard,' he hissed. 'Ought to be hanged by ——,' and he mentioned a portion of the human anatomy about which it would have been difficult if not impossible to fasten a rope.

Katie had, of course, found it impossible to keep even the most menial of jobs, and despite the fact she laughed incessantly, she must have been aware that the future held nothing for her and the chances were she would hang on Annie's apron strings until Annie became too infirm to work the fruit fields or follow the potato harvester. Mumpers, as a whole, seem to be a curious section of society who usually work until they are unable, finally falling into a state of wretchedness that attracts the interest of social workers, who feel it a kindness to clean up the near-senile often prematurely aged mumpers, put them in clean, respectable institutions, where in such sterile and antiseptic environments, the mumpers invariably fade away and die. Since meeting the band, I've met and talked with several groups of mumpers, all of whom live in terror of being 'put in a home'. Annie lived in dread of the time when she would be unable to work and the infantile Katie would be taken from her, but neither the smelly, eneuretic Annie nor the feeble-minded Katie qualified for the title of the most wretched of the group.

Megan had remained silent during the discussion around that furze and railway sleeper fire, scarcely touching her mess of potato, onion, and corned beef hash, her knees held close to her emaciated bust by scrawny claw-like hands, rocking to and fro like the inmate of a Jack London home for the feeble-minded, or a person suffering from catatonia. Annie explained the tale of the wretched paper-thin-skinned woman, and as the ancient Annie spoke, I stared at Megan realising that with the weather getting colder by the day, she would certainly not be able to stand the rigours of the oncoming winter or even complete the potato harvest. I continued to stare at her, musing over what I considered a clever epigram that the Third World began at Fort William, and the do-gooders of this world, the pro-Oxfam-help-the-deprived would do well to begin the programme at this half-acre of mud and ashes near opulent Fort William. I shuddered slightly as I saw myself broken by the social requirements of teaching, forced to opt out and live the way of these people. Megan was unable to take the life and the hardships and I felt damned sure that devoid of employment and financial help, neither would I. The wretched Megan was, according to

Annie, a native of West Wales, and had married a village boy whom she had known since childhood. He had a powerful tenor voice of the type regularly produced by that particular area and, after a scholarship to a college of music, he seemed to have made a success of the world of opera and oratorio, and outgrown his village wife and her two-year-old daughter, moving to a world of Mozart and Berlioz, finding solace in the arms of contraltos and sopranos. His wife, in a village where divorce was still considered scandalous, had taken the break-up of her marriage badly, and after teetering on the brink of insanity, had tried to gas herself and the child. It was an unsuccessful attempt at suicide, and the authorities had taken both into custody, releasing the still-demented Megan, perhaps prematurely, but fostering out the child to a safer, if not a more caring home. Perhaps, only perhaps, a string of unfortunate affairs had followed in the wake of her release, perhaps each lover seedier, coarser, rougher, less socially acceptable than the last, as she slithered down the precipitous slope from respectability. Finally this pitiful, anorexic wretch found herself homeless and wandering the countryside, joining up with similar dispirited social rejects, each one in his or her own way equally as unhappy as Megan. As she rocked to and fro, I became aware that she was not really staring into the campfire which lit up the wagon of decaying, sodden bed clothes and mattresses, but was instead in her neat and comfy kitchen back in Cardigan, her child playing on the linoleum and her husband practising for the local oratorio. A gust of wind fanned the campfire creating a fresh flame and the blaze lit up Megan's face revealing a smile on her white lips. To awaken her, to bring her back from the cosy respectability of her Welsh kitchen, would have been sacrilege and everyone, even the awful Bomber, was prepared to let her dwell in her quaint, nicer-than-nice, sing-song-voice, Welsh world of Oz. From time to time Annie hugged the skeleton figure as if to give her some sense of affection, some feeling of security perhaps, though security seemed a star's flight away from that filthy hovel-like railway carriage on the side of a bleak and windswept hill in Scotland.

I tried to shut Megan out of my mind and turned to the powerfully built figure of Johnny.

'Why do they call you Johnny Walker?' I asked. 'Have you', I toyed desperately with a suitable expression, but came out with simply, 'a drink problem?'

He laughed the sound coming from within the cavity of his chest.

'No, not now,' he added, perhaps a shade wistfully.

'Johnny's been to the Universal,' put in Annie proudly as though the presence of an intellectual gave a veneer of class to the pathetic little band.

Johnny winked as if to acknowledge Annie's malapropism, and gave a rapid if not staccato curriculum vitae.

'I read biology, taught a while, fought pro and bounced in and out of a sort of marriage.'

He saw my raised eyebrow at the mention of a 'sort' of marriage.

'I made some hapless lass pregnant, married her on the agreement that she went away and I've never seen her since,' he shrugged. 'Perhaps for the best, considering the circumstances,' Johnny added a shade bitterly.

'I fought until I was twenty-eight and went on a drinking rampage when I realised I was over the top. Hell, it was some rampage. Could not keep a job, drunk day and night, a slippery slope down which all I could do was roll. Ever been on a bender?'

I nodded.

'Well, I awoke up one morning to find myself lying in the gutter with some loon pissing over me and his idiot friends laughing. Enough was enough after that. I dried out quickly, and painfully,' he added, 'and haven't touched the stuff since. The nickname "Johnny Walker"? Well, I go everywhere on foot. Time is about the only thing of which I've plenty.'

He eyed the band, shaking his head as he did so. Bomber was hacking the log madly, Jimmy limply trying to scrabble a potato out of the ashes, and Katie actively engaged in picking her nose, a look of near ecstacy spreading across her face.

'This isn't rock bottom,' he muttered noting perhaps my pained expression. 'Take my word for it,' he continued, 'I've been there. At least these are still eager to hang on to life for what it's worth. I reached the stage where it wasn't worth hanging on, so every step of the way back is a bonus.'

'I know,' I said quietly, 'I'm at the bottom of the heap myself.'

My intention of explaining my sad and wretched lot in life was thwarted by Annie, a born if somewhat smelly organiser who, aware of the feeling of melancholy which was beginning to pervade the group, spoke up sharply.

'Right – it's still early like. What shall we do afore bed time? Ain't go no teles here, Mister, got to make our own fun. Megan, Megan love, give us a tune.'

At first I was amazed at Annie for chiding the silent, anorexic woman who had contributed nothing to the conversation or the making of the meal, but to my amazement the zombie-like Megan arose and, in an astonishingly strong voice, sang 'When the Stars were Brightly Shining' from Puccini's *Tosca*. Her voice resounded across the bleak and silent countryside, startling even the sneering and sniggering Jamie to silence, and I noticed that Jimmy had desisted from spitting into the fire, and Bomber had taken a temporary respite from hacking at his railway sleeper. Megan finished her song abruptly, squatted down on her haunches and began rocking to and fro again. How apt, yet inapt, the choice of song was. She sang it in excellent Italian – a man's solo she had heard her husband rehearse a hundred times or more, the song of Rudolph, a political refugee, as much a refugee as Megan was from the hostile world of reality. I think I must have smiled to myself and shaken my head. It was Puccini who had once said, 'When I am not in love, then hold my funeral', and the passion of Megan's song made me realise that Megan still loved this man who perhaps at that very moment in time was partaking of a champagne dinner completely oblivious to the fact that his one-time wife was living in wretched freezing squalor somewhere in the Highlands.

A silence followed the ending of Megan's song, a silence broken only by Annie in her MC's capacity.

'Well, who's next to do some entertaining? Bomber?'

Bomber snapped back to his nasty, ferocious self.

'Piss off, shit bag.'

'Hardly entertaining,' countered Johnny quietly, and I sensed the frightening antipathy between the cool and calm opted-out academic, and the vicious misanthrope, hacking the railway sleeper with his broken Bowie knife. Jimmy spat loudly on the fire and the sizzling sound seemed to break the awful tension around the camp fire.

Annie, unperturbed by the seething ferocity of Bomber, turned to me, 'Go on, you're a schoolmister. You tell us a tale. Schoolmisters is always good at stories.'

Curiously, I was good at story telling, about my only gift teaching-wise I suppose, and immediately I stood and told the tale of Sindbad and his meeting with the Old Man of the Sea, a monstrous demon creature which persuaded sailors to allow him to sit on their shoulders, whereupon he began to throttle the life out of his victims. Sindbad alone unseats him by getting him drunk, and once the old man has slid from Sindbad's shoulders, pounding the life out of the demon with a large rock.

'S'great tale,' clapped Annie.

'Is it true? Is it true?' trilled Katie, while Bomber snarling afresh, began to hack more savagely than ever at the railway sleeper, ripping, gutting, slicing into the Old Man of the Sea (or perhaps Johnny).

I felt pleased with myself. I considered myself a good spinner of yarns, a fair teller of tales, but my story paled to insignificance when it became Johnny's turn to entertain us.

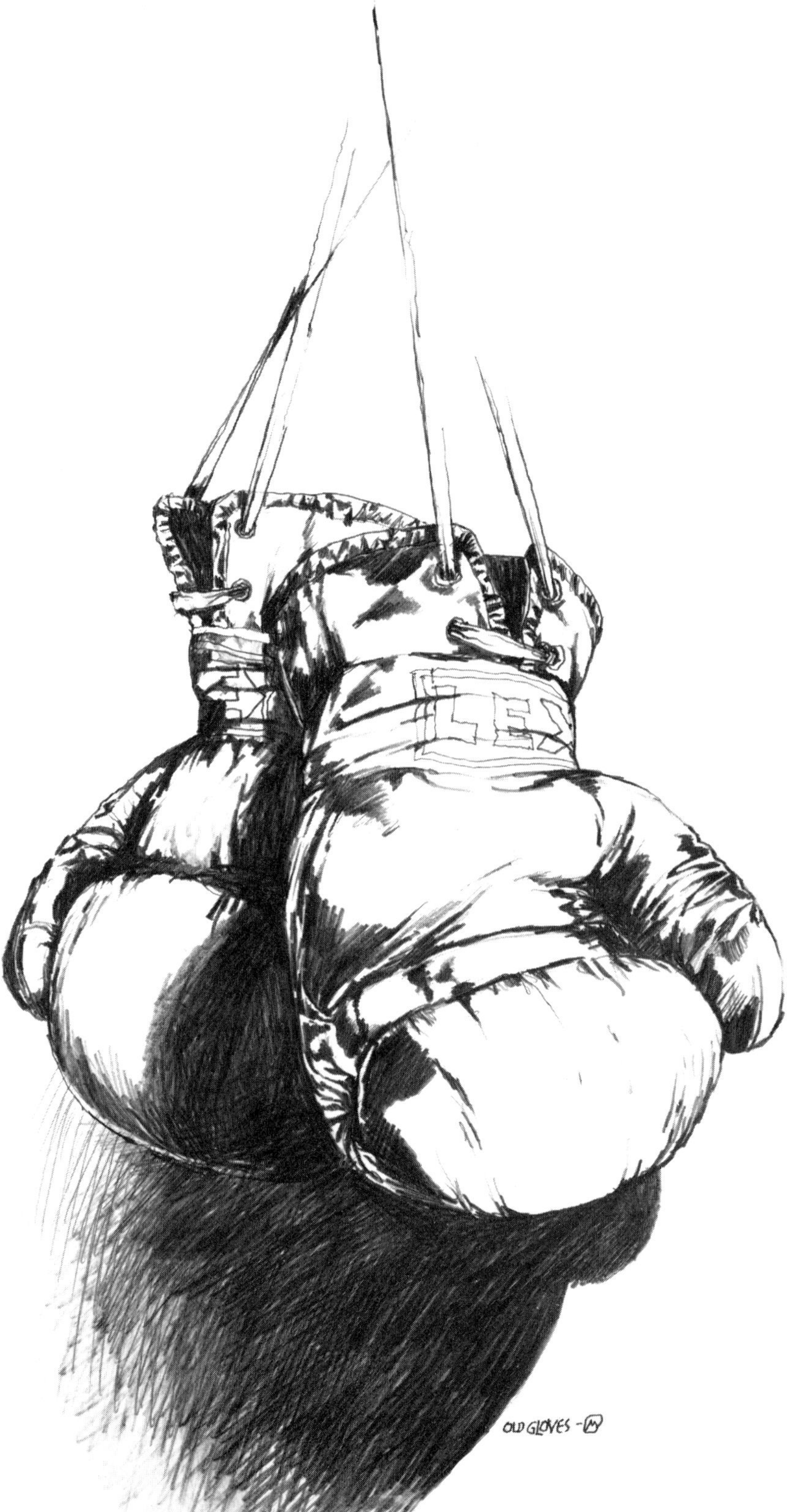
OLD GLOVES -

—6—

Johnny's Tale

THE FIRE LIT up the faces of the ragtag and bobtail audience gathered around that fireside as Johnny began his story.

I always find the statement, 'Pain is only in the mind', a little hard to understand, he said quietly, and question whether the person uttering such a statement has experienced pain – and by pain I don't mean a minor ache like a sprained ankle or an abscess in the gums, but real pain, the sort that makes the very fibres of one's body scream out as if they too wish to be released from the structure which is holding them together. Pain of this nature is real, it is nothing to do with being in the mind and is so tangible as to allow a man to reach out and touch the very perimeter of the pain that is exuding from a point in his body.

At the time when I first formulated this theory I was maybe twenty-eight years old, long past my best as a middle-weight. Ten years before, some of the press had hailed me as a future world champion after a few hasty moderately skilful, but mostly lucky and quick wins. It was a premature prediction, a reckless stab at stardom, but it made me feel good, warm inside, confident of every battle, and such confidence carried me through five or six hard struggles until I too became a little doubtful that I was world class. After my first loss, a blistering, hurting six-rounder against an experienced fighter, who was going nowhere and climbing down the rungs of the ladder of stardom, a few friends tried to cheer me up by remarking that Louis had dropped a decision to Schmelling and Greb had given Tunney a boxing lesson, but it was I who was going into the ring, dishing out, and now receiving punishing head and body shots, and it was I who was aware that I was not the stuff of which champions are made.

A fighter with his brain still functioning in his head, gets to know the signs that he is on the way out fairly quickly. Training becomes slightly irksome, less of a joy than it was during the winning years, and there is a certain dullness that pervades the once electrically charged atmosphere of the changing room just prior to a fight. The crowd seem no longer to be 'rooting' for you and the roars and yells which accompany one of your increasingly rare punch and counter-punch flurries seem to be softer, less enthusiastic than the shouts one hears when one's opponent's attacks are ripping home. A fighter, one with an ounce of sense, not the punch-drunk fool who hangs around gyms hoping some mug will sponsor his comeback, is aware of his loss of form, his gradual decline, long before even the sharpest manager or promoter and knows it is time to get out, to nail up his gloves before slurred speech, double vision and inability to concentrate tells the audience the fighter is, to use fight parlance, a bum.

By my twenty-third birthday I realised I wasn't going to be a champion and long before my twenty-fourth I knew it was time to quit. However, when the time came, when I knew it was right to hang up my gloves, and announce my retirement like Bedevere reluctant to cast away the sword Excalibur, somehow I just couldn't do it. I'd had a university education, but I'd failed to stick at any job which even smacked of anything academic, and I'd been in the fight game since the day after my twelfth birthday. To hand in my licence was a little like asking a swallow to stop flying, and though the roar of the crowd no longer rooted for me and old men in public houses talked about me as 'one who'd been a good un in his day', I refrained from announcing my retirement.

The way down is interesting in a sort of peculiar way and fascinating to watch. The 'has been' notes, and notes fairly quickly, that during his bout the audience are trickling out to the bar to get stocked up before the 'important' battle, and a glance at the fight bill posters finds one's name in smaller letters and lower down the lists of gladiators. Programmes tell the fighter most, however, for whereas they describe in glowing eulogies the merits of those who are top of the bill, the on-the-way-out fighter is always described briefly, perhaps a little too briefly, as a 'crowd pleaser' sure to please or if things have taken a temporary turn for the better, 'put up a great fight in this hall last month'. Turns for the better are short-lived however, and slowly but surely one becomes a joke figure, a chopping block on which every up-and-coming fighter, every battler with hope, ambition and vitality, and the glow of expectant stardom are tested. It's time to quit then, or maybe join the band of disfigured, damaged, dispirited, ex-pugs which haunt every gym and training room from Birmingham to Bangkok.

On my twenty-eighth birthday, I reflected on my life. Jersey Joe Walcott had won the heavy-weight championship of the world when he was thirty-eight, but unlike Jersey Joe I had lost ten decisions in a row and even my friends in the press were urging me to hang up my gloves before it was 'too late'. Some nights I'd be lucky enough to get a fight – usually as a substitute for some athlete who'd injured a hand at the last moment or 'scratched' through a severe head cold. More often than not, however, I'd earn a few pounds sparring with an up-and-coming boy enduring, though not enjoying, the new head and body shots which his trainer was teaching him on a living punch bag. By day I worked as a hod carrier, a crippling job, hard on the arm, back and harder still on the soul. Some evenings I'd ached so much I didn't even feel the arm punches some good prospect was getting in on me when he pinned me in a corner. In trade terms, I'd become a 'bag carrier' – a down and out, willing, more than willing, to black the shoes of any boy good enough to go in the ring, if only to smell the acrid stench of punch-drawn sweat and hear the roar of the crowd.

Funnily enough, my big chance came that year. A British boxer had high-tailed it up the ladder of success to a world title shot to be fought in Sicks Stadium, Seattle – a gold-spangled pleasure dome where Marciano, Sugar Ray, Mohammed Ali, and a hundred other greats had battled, and a score of ambitions had been granted or dashed to pieces in the twenty-four foot ring under the blinding lights of the stadium. A fighter going for a world title shot doesn't go it alone without a backup team. A host of followers accompany him, Ray Robinson's crowd were called a circus and the name seems to have stuck ever since. As luck would have it I was picked as one of the circus, a general 'go for', a boot boy, a bag carrier, and at a pinch a sparring partner to sharpen up our boy just before the fight, a sort of punch-bag who could be relied on not to hurt the Golden Boy during sparring and still endure a rain of blows. A stroke of luck I called it at the time, and jumped at the chance, yet luck has always had a funny way of ill-treating me throughout my forty-odd years of life.

Our would-be champion was booked into some marbled halls hotel while the rest of us scoured the city for rooms. I came to rest in a flea-ridden little ten by ten room across the hall from a Turkish landlord and below the rooms of a lady who specialised in entertaining men who took a great deal of pleasure in inflicting pain and maybe a few other less pleasant things besides. I lay on my bed most evenings, and worked out, did 'go for' jobs and sparred a little in the two weeks before the fight. Seattle looked hostile, particularly to a down-at-heel like me and I had no real wish to see the sights outside the pleasure dome.

Our boy came on well and, as he keyed for the big fight his punches went in harder with more precision, with more deliberation, and with more intent to cause pain. A sparring partner takes the rough with the smooth, some aspiring champions take it easy on a training target, others are out to hurt, to test their own 'hitting power', to prepare themselves for the big night, and to test to the utmost every new punch they intended to use on the big fight. Our boy set out to hurt, and each and every sparring partner began to complain of the punishment he took during those gruelling bouts. Some nights I felt so sore I couldn't lie on my left side, but dawn and the roadsweeper found both the contender and I pounding the streets of Seattle, watched by wakening down-and-outs and curious cops working out the last minutes of their beat.

The big night came and we sat in the changing rooms making idle and stupid chatter to put our boy at ease, while our trainer rubbed and oiled him, caressing his back and body with the same love and care as a mother might a baby. I glanced up and smiled a wry and bitter grin as I remembered when I too merited such treatment, but it was a long time ago and the feeling was hard as hell to recall. I snapped out of my reverie when a trilby-hatted, skinny little guy who looked like the cartoon of one Scoop Morgan, ace reporter, burst into the dressing room and shouted in panic, 'Number five is out. Christ sake, anyone who can even touch welter or even middle among you crowd of bums?' I felt the eyes turn to me. I shook my head. 'I'm two and half pounds over middle and I'm nowhere near fit.' 'You'll do,' yelled the guy in the trilby, but I shook my head dismissing the idea. 'Look,' he went on, getting more excited by the minute, 'there's $200 in it, no, make it $300 if you put up a show, and we'll drop the eight 3-minute rounds to six 2-minutes.' I glanced at the programme. The fifth bout was Cortez Luis, a welter-weight coming in nearly two stone below me weight-wise. I'd seen his name often enough in *Boxing News* and he was after Ortega's crown. He'd notched twenty-eight wins to his credit, five of his opponents had gone the distance but the others he'd bludgeoned, butchered, battered and cut into submission well before the final bell. He'd been matched with a boy from Detroit who'd come in at number eight in the world ratings, but anyone with half an eye could see the fight was simply a warm-up for the Ortega battle. Ortega was thirty-four, well-worn, past his prime, a ripe plum simply hanging from the tree and Luis was scheduled to be the picker. 'Come on, make up your frigging mind. Do you want the money or not?' Scoop Morgan snapped. Three hundred dollars – on my last fight I'd taken a terrific beating for eight pounds! I felt the electrically charged atmosphere fill the room yet once more, and after studying Scoop Morgan's face for a minute or so I nodded and he raced off to amend the contract.

I changed, noting my poor physical shape in the mirror, and received a cursory rub down with spirit while I lay face down on the table. It was, I felt, a token gesture. I wasn't expected to win or even last the distance. I can remember the comments of my fellow sparring partners – and one, just one, remarked, 'You've never been stopped, have you?' I shook my head, hoping that the butterflies in my stomach, signs that tell a fighter he is keyed up, would appear, but they didn't. I wasn't ready for the fight either mentally or physically, and I was well aware the boy I was to fight was well out of my class – a star's flight above me in fact, and that the battle about to be fought would finish up as a ridiculous travesty, not a warm-up fight for a world title shot.

He was already in the ring when I climbed through the ropes and limbering up. Somehow I couldn't take him seriously, despite his awesome record. He looked like a dancer from *West Side Story* rather than a potential world welter-weight – a finely proportioned slim-hipped, light, mobile-shouldered boy who played with a rosary as he prepared for the oncoming battle. We came to the centre of the ring and the ref, a Chilian or Argentinian, went through the rules in English, and then began to recite the regulations in Spanish. Luis stopped him gently, 'I speak English', he half-whispered, and returned to his corner, knelt a second, handed his rosary to his trainer and then the mockery began.

We touched gloves and I watched him, gauging his stance, his eyes, his body movement as we circled, deciding who should land the first blow. He was no longer the effete dancer of a Broadway musical, but a silent, soft-moving, light-footed feline, a cat-like beast weighing up the prowess of a kill rather than the style of an opponent. He took my first blows, parrying them easily, knowing I was a short-time substitute, aware that I couldn't hurt him, and his initial flurry flung with contemptuous care caught me unawares, rocking me against the ropes, making my head reel. My blows, my best punches, simply connected with his arms or his gloves, and he continued to jab and hack where and when he wanted to. It became a game to him, an extension of a sparring bout and he knew I presented no danger to him despite my extra weight. His fists beat a steady rat-tat-tat on my ribs and once, and only once, when I tried a heavy head shot he slid effortlessly back out of range, his face stony and expressionless, yet oddly youth-like.

The second, third, and fourth rounds followed the same ridiculous pattern. He had no desire to finish the fight for there was no glory in defeating a substitute – a nobody who had come in with the circus of an aspiring champion. He took ridiculous chances, exposing his vital points and sliding gracefully and contemptuously out of the way when I tried to follow up. He regarded me as a joke perhaps as a hundred other fighters had regarded me, but somehow his attitude, his demeanour had begun to anger me. To lose one's temper in the ring is the surest way to defeat, for it leaves one's body and head open to the easiest of blows, the most rudimentary of shots. I had never lost my temper during my 148 bouts and had fought too many colours and creeds to be a racist, but now my mind was filled with an almost insane hatred to hurt or damage this damnable little spick who danced around me, treating me like a first-time-out amateur, making me look ridiculous, more foolish than I'd ever looked before. I tried every shot I knew on him, every dodge, every trick in the book, picked up in a hundred rings all over Europe, but he simply parried them or danced out of the way. The mad desire to hurt him, to kill him if need be, swept over me and during the fifth round I fouled him repeatedly, bringing my head up into his face to cut an eye, break a nose, inflict any wound I could, but although he glanced across at the ref, he said nothing, and simply moved his head out of the range of my butting action. I switched to the body, hitting him as low as I could, twice feeling my glove hit his groin guard, but once again he swayed out of distance, glancing at the ref perhaps, but saying nothing. Half-way through the round he closed with me in the centre of the ring and almost whispered, 'I'm sorry.'

An explosion hit me below the ribs on my left hand side, an awful sunburst, the sensation of a cannonball ripping into my flesh, jarring the breath from my body, filling every fibre of my chest cavity with twisting, writhing agony. I'd sucked air desperately and my zoology training made me realise that his blow had driven the fundus of my stomach upwards, rupturing the diaphragm, and creating a massive hiatus hernia. He stepped back and walked to a neutral corner while I fell on my knees, hung on the ropes, desperately sucking air.

I stared across the ring, watching a pool of mist-like ectoplasm seep from my injured side, trying to gather it in with my gloves, convinced that should it leave my body completely I would die. The pool extended and panic overcame me, yet the count of the ref became amazingly slow, not the rapid one-to-ten count over a boy who has taken a bad head shot. I scooped the pool towards me, hearing my seconds whisper, 'Stay down, he'll kill you', but though my body and mind knew that there was safety and possibly life on that canvas floor, my legs accustomed to fifteen hard-fought years in the ring, refused to obey. 'Seven', and I felt my body begin to straighten, and by 'nine' I had staggered to my feet. The bell clanged mercifully perhaps out of pity as I staggered to my corner.

'You're shot, you've had it,' my seconds went on. 'For Christ sake, don't touch my side,' I almost screamed, as they poured water down my trunks. The ref strolled over and asked how I was and was I ready to continue. I nodded, knowing that a 'Yes' would start up the agony again. 'Throw in the towel and I'll kill you, you bastard,' I spat at my second as the final round began.

We touched gloves and he smiled slightly, not the condescending smile of a victor who stood over a vanquished prey, of an Achilles over a fallen Hector, but a smile that smacked almost of friendship. I hung close to him, waltzed him, knowing that another blow so delivered would kill me, but while he made a few head shots, they were with the slapping action of the glove, blows not designed to hurt, noisy shots more for the audience than the referee. For two long minutes he let me hold on, allowing me to use his body as a prop lest I should fall. At no time could he have not finished me, brutally beaten me, cut me, torn me, killed me, yet he allowed those two endless minutes to continue. The bell rang and the ref instantly raised Luis's hand in victory.

He came to my corner and kissed both cheeks as a father might kiss a recalcitrant child he has just reluctantly spanked. 'I am sorry,' he said. 'Forgive me, but my fight with Ortega was at stake.' I nodded, aware that speech would be an agony and watched him don his dressing gown and slip carelessly through the ropes. I crawled back to the dressing rooms, vomiting shamelessly, despite the jeers of the crowd and the rain of Pepsi-cola cans.

That night I spent vomiting into the basin in my ten-by-ten hovel while the lady upstairs screamed and roared as a particularly active client went to work on her, but all my Turkish landlord could think of was hammering on my door and shouting 'Drunken limey bastard – I want you out of here in the morning, pronto.'

I lost my hod-carrying job when I returned to England and laid up for a month living on my purse money, eating little and often to allow my frightful injury to heal. At the end of the month, providing I watched my diet, I kept my food down with only a little discomfort, but the bout finished my career in the square ring.

Luis got his fight with Ortega, but the outcome was not what was expected. No one favoured the reigning champion and it was a forgone conclusion that Luis would be the next world welter-weight. Somehow things didn't pan out as predicted. For four rounds Luis pushed the aged champion around like a doll, treating him like a joke, hitting him where and when he wanted. In the fifth round, Ortega landed a blow high on Luis's head, and the challenger fell heavily to the canvas. He never regained consciousness and died two days later.

I'd forgotten about the fight and was back teaching again and involved in an affair with a lady doctor. The word 'affair' is a bit of a misnomer, for on our first date she prepared curry and dutifully I ate it. Seconds later I was in agony, vomiting down the toilet. She watched critically. 'You've a hiatus hernia, haven't you?' she asked sharply. I nodded, still vomiting. 'How did you get it?' she continued blissfully, unaware I was unable to answer. 'Boxing,' I gasped. She stood hands on hips and went into a diatribe against the sport. 'How a grown man can stand there and allow another to punch him so hard as to create a hiatus hernia beats me.' 'You should see the other chap,' I tried to joke, but the irony was missed on her, and besides that, I never saw her again.

Johnny ended his tale quietly poking the fire with a stick until the sparks had flown upwards and the flames had lit the Decameron-type figures seated around the camp fire. Johnny's story, told with a professional touch, had nevertheless fallen on deaf ears. Katie, the imbecile Katie, had fallen asleep and Annie had to restrain her to prevent her toppling into the fire. Bomber had exhausted himself with his constant hacking action and now stared moodily into the fire of furze. Jimmy was giving the fire his last spit of the evening and Megan was quietly smiling to herself, whispering endearments in Welsh and at the campsite in body only. Jamie was munching into his staple diet of glucose, milk and whatever else is the component of a Mars Bar, washing the gooey mess down with slurps of McEwan's.

'A great tale,' I complimented Johnny, 'a great tale.' I felt embarrassed. 'Look, if any of you are near Lichfield, just call in and see me.'

Johnny came nearer to the fire and the flames lit up his face now almost laconic in expression.

'Would you really want the likes of us near your respectable little home.' he sneered, 'or are you preparing yourself for a pariah life style of the type we lead?'

He walked towards the railway carriage and lay down on his sacks of bracken as far from the evil-smelling Annie as possible, next to the formidable Bomber, who was now asleep, still caressing the broken Bowie knife, and grunting angrily in his awful sleep.

'Think about it,' Johnny said quietly, and turned over, falling asleep instantly, grunting and snoring as loudly as the rest of the band.

'I'll be sleeping in the van with you,' Jamie stated rather than asked.

I erupted out of my pensive mood. 'Listen, you burk, I know that they are probably covered in lice and fleas, but the stench coming from you night and day is ghastly, and frankly I'm brassed off with you and your stinking little habits.'

'Tain't the fleas that worry me, mate, no way,' Jamie replied with a shrug of his shoulders. 'Bomber noticed I got two cans of McEwan's in the van and he'll be after these like . . .' he reached for a smile, 'a rat up a drain pipe,' he settled for. 'Too right, he will!'

We were gone before any of the mumpers had awoken and were clanging and clattering north to Ullapool in the cold spell which followed shortly after that depressing autumnal dawn.

THE ONE-EYED TOM

—7—

Another Cup of Tea Mr er. . . Palmer

'ANOTHER CUP OF tea, Mr er . . . Palmer?' I was jolted back reluctantly to semi-wakefulness by the antique Mrs Richardson, a three times widowed octogenarian who kept a bed and breakfast house on the way to fashionable Ullapool, a tourist town which harboured a mixed collection of camera-carrying American tourists, literally rubbing shoulders with almost Asiatic-looking Russian fishermen from the trawlers anchored discretely in the bay.

I had, to quote a scornful Jamie, been 'driven in', forced to take refuge in a bed and breakfast house, not because of the inclement weather and the fact that my van heater was on the blink, but simply because after four days on the road I stank. I am forced to admit that I am none too fragrant at the best of times even though I bath daily, and now after four days in the company of Jamie and a chance encounter with the mumper band, I felt decidedly dirty. I bought some Bob Martin's Flea Powder at a chemist's shop in Fort William, ostensibly to clear Penguin and Fathom of unwanted visitors, but within minutes of leaving the camp I was aware that I was host to a myriad of parasites which caused me to scratch constantly until even the equally fragrant, and certainly equally verminous Jamie remarked none too politely on my habit of non-stop scratching. Thus it was at the first bed and breakfast house, and the Highlands boast thousands of such places, I booked in to bath, de-louse myself and for the first time in nearly a week sleep in a clean proper bed. Jamie, still nursing his cans of McEwan's and sporting a bundle of fivers still big enough to choke a cow, was adamant in his refusal to, I quote, 'pay for a night's bleeding kip'. 'Besides that,' he put in, 'the woman's daft about cats.' He referred of course to the Roald Dahl figure of Mrs Richardson for Jamie seemed to know just about everyone on that road running up the West Coast of Scotland.

I had tapped on the door of an antiquated-looking house, the garden of which boasted a score of cottage garden plants, which had gone out of fashion during my grandfather's day, and despite my appearance – I looked decidedly wretched – and the fact that most houses were closed now that the season had finished, Mrs Richardson, obviously a lady who liked human company, had welcomed me in. I explained my need for a bath, none too graphically of course and now after bathing, de-lousing and de-fleaing myself with Bob Martin's Flea Powder (extra strength), I was sitting in Mrs Richardson's warm and comfy parlour and dozing off to sleep. The elderly white-haired lady nudged me to consciousness with an offer of tea and yet another scone. I declined graciously, I hope, and steeled myself for another conversational attack for Mrs Richardson was, as Jamie said, 'daft about cats'.

I've always lived a bachelor life punctuated with a series of very ephemeral affairs and I've come to the conclusion that to preserve any state of normality, a bachelor or any single person for that matter, should keep his animals out of doors. Frankly there isn't such a thing as a totally house-trained animal, for every beast no matter how fastidious its toilet habits, leaves a trail of itself around the house and in next to no time one's residence develops a decidely doggy or worse still catty smell. Mrs Richardson was an immaculately clad old lady, white-haired, white-pinafored with whiter than white tablecloths and a Jane Austin type of cleanliness, but her interest in cats was hard to conceal as soon as she opened her front door.

'Did I tell you how I got Peter?' Mrs Richardson continued to refer to how she had achieved ownership of one hopefully neutered, one-eyed, moth-eaten tom-cat who had surreptitiously tried to bat my scone from my plate with its four-clawed paw, while I hypocritically feigned interest, hoping that sleep would not overtake the fascinating narrative of Peter. Mrs Richardson had dozens of cats, and the acquisition of every cat held a tale. Each and every cat had been acquired by some considerable effort by Mrs Richardson. Each and every hideously ancient moggy was loved, cherished and had been rescued from a life of lean feral freedom by the auspices of the good lady and now that the season had ended and there were no tourists to regale with her tales of feline filching, one D. B. Plummer otherwise known as Mr er Mr Palmer, was selected to be the recipient of Mrs Richardson's tales of monstrous moggies and curious cats.

The good lady droned on about her cats and the ways they were acquired while I drifted off into reverie, smiling occasionally and probably inanely just to prove I was conscious and still listening. It was a knack I had developed in school staff meetings held by extra-boring headmasters who droned on incessantly about nothing in particular and took an hour to say something which an ill-educated docker could have said in ten words, four of which were four-letter expletives. After years of teaching, a captive teacher learns to smile, simper and nod – nodding is absolutely essential – in the right places. To return to Mrs Richardson, who although boring, was far more interesting than most meeting-holding headmasters I have met.

People really do go over the top about cats, daft in fact, and even soap opera fans, 'hooked' so to speak on Coronation Street have been known to lose touch with the dirty goings on at the Rovers Return and switch over to watch a programme on the humble fireside moggy. Early Celtic students and monks wrote poems about them. T. S. Eliot scribed a nonsense book of verse about them and Andrew Lloyd Webber made a fortune setting the selfsame nonsense poems to music, playing to packed houses every night, and calling his musical rather appropriately *Cats*. The Egyptians who really were cat daft were probably the first to keep cats, if cats can be kept for they seem to go where they wish and when they wish. Lorenz, who is a Nobel Prize winner, and therefore should know, believes that while man deliberately set about domesticating the dog, the cat, the African wildcat to be precise, a species related to the European wildcat but considerably tamer, was attracted to early Egyptian dwelling places by the presence of rodent vermin (rats and mice), which had lived a life of Riley on the grain stores for which Egypt was at one time famous. Whatever – within a matter of a few years of cats seeking to pal up with rodent-over-run man, the Egyptians had become well and truly cat crazy and even set to embalming the cats (hopefully after death) and placing them alongside the mummies of their owners. It is said the Egyptians actually worshipped a cat-god called Bas, which seems very likely as they had a variety of gods ranging from hippos to hawks which goes to show the early Egyptians were a funny lot – religious, but a bit funny if you ask me.

After Egypt started to expand its Empire, cats started popping up in a variety of places and in a variey of guises. In Persia, hence I suppose Persian cats, long-haired editions of the African wildcat appeared and after Alexander literally stamped the life out of the Persians, cats were taken back to Greece and hence to the rest of Europe. The Egyptians, however, seem to be the very last people to be able to train cats and there are drawings found on ancient tombs of Egyptians hunting marsh birds with cats – or at least hunters accompanied by tabby-striped cats.

Tabby – now there's a word with which to toy. The word is apparently Turkish though nearly every type of wildcat in Europe and North Africa is tabby coloured. Wildcat – an untamable sort of person like McCauley's Horatious who 'like a wildcat mad of wounds sprang into Astur's face'. The African wildcat was or is a relatively easily tamed beast but the European wildcat, broader of head, shorter of tail, is a different ball game. If you were to pick up a wildcat kitten straight out of the nest, if the dam isn't about (you'll be in for a hell of a bad time if she is), rear it with the tamest available she-cat you can find and breed from it, three generations later the kittens are still as wild as hawks. When I was a lad of about twelve, I'd been to see the Shropshire naturalist called Frances Pitt and she'd really researched felis sylvestris grampiensis (the wildcat of the Scottish woods). Miss Pitt had not only bred pure wildcats, but she'd also crossed the males with tame females, and the resulting kittens were not only stumpy-tailed, but also as fierce as their sires and completely untamable.

Hybrids abound in the cat world. At one time, I used to spend a few pounds a month buying American sporting periodicals, massive affairs large enough to put *Field* and *Country Life* to shame, and so crammed with fascinating facts that by the time I'd finished reading one, the next had arrived by post. The Americans are great people for owning unusual pets – every Walt Disney family household seems to be choc full of critters – and adverts for puma, ocelot and jaguar cubs abounded (until the 1974 Act, you could buy them in Britain). More interesting still were the hybrids twixt ocelot and tame cat, and very fierce margay (small ocelots) and tame cats. Perhaps such hybrids are still for sale. I lost my job teaching, not an unusual event, took a drop in salary and didn't renew my subscription to the magazines. Not that I wanted to buy an ocelot hybrid mind you, though I did once visit a man who bred servals (bat-eared, leggy African middle-sized cats) and owned a very tame female (who had lost her leg in a trap), and a far from tame male. The kittens were a shade too old to handle by the time I saw them. Pity – though I don't really get on with things feline.

Howell Dda (Howell the Good) did. He was a Welsh king who knew just about everybody and wrote just about everything. He estimated that a good cat, one which killed mice and didn't eat its kittens, was well worth having, so worthwhile in fact that anyone who killed such a cat paid a curious type of compensation to the agrieved cat owner. The cat was hung down till its nose touched the floor and a load of grain, enough to bury the cat, tipped over the beast – just about 3 cwt of dry grain seemed to be enough. Funnily enough, I've always questioned whether Howell the Good wrote these curious laws or existed for that matter, yet most books quote him verbatim and never even question him.

Yet cats weren't always held in high esteem. About five hundred years after Howell the Good – who probably didn't exist – a pair of monkish gentlemen called Sprenger and Kramer certainly did exist. Both were sadists of the first order and worse still religious maniacs, for good old-fashioned sadists know roughly when to stop their unpleasant little capers and the victim lives to walk, or at least limp, away from the encounter, but a religious maniac with sadistic intentions goes the whole hog firmly convinced that the agony he or she is inflicting is for the victim's good. Hence, hideous tortures are perpetrated in the name of religion. Personally, I am a little against Christianity and think there is something unwholesome about a church which sports effigies showing the dying body of a man nailed to a cross in every nook and cranny. Be that as it may, and it's sure to offend someone. Sprenger and Kramer went one step further than even the most obsessive sadist, for the goodly pair saw evil whence and where they looked and being as they were actively looking they came up with some pretty astounding conclusions. Europe, or so the pair believed, seemed to be populated with a liberal sprinkling of werewolves, witches and warlocks with a soupçon of vampires thrown in for good measure, with just the odd normal peasant or so to work the land. Clearly the pair were bats – but the Pope who was equally peculiar, believed the pair implicitly and promoted their wares and encouraged them to put together a bumper fun book called *Malleus Malificorum*, The Hammer of the Witches, an indispensable piece of literature if one thought one's neighbour was out cavorting in the guise of a werewolf or, like the curious lady fluttering around the room describing how she'd had the good fortune to come by a mangy moggy called Chloe (part Siamese I believe), was 'bats about cats'. Apparently, according to Sprenger and Kramer – it's never been proved scientifically, witches who were not very keen on being found out (and with madmen like the demonic duo hunting them, who would be?), simply sent a spirit enclosed in the body of a black dog or worse still in a cat to suss out the landscape and find someone to hurt. God help the poor unfortunates who kept two or more cats, or an old lady like Mrs Richardson who saw it as her life's duty to find and care for any stray cat in the district. God help them, though if medieval accounts are correct, he seldom did. I looked up and in my mind's eye saw the immaculate and respectable old lady still wearing a snow-white pinafore, burning at the stake, the fibres of which were fuelled and stoked by Hammer-House-of-Horror extras obligatorily clad in Bavarian costumes (even if the film was set in Britain). Funnily enough, the madness escaped Britain until James I of England came to the throne and having Scottish parents and a continental education, could have been expected to be a little on the 'rare' side anyway. He fulfilled everyone's expectations by plagiarizing the good works, or simply copying the notes and writing an equally tripe-ridden epic called *Demonology* – as neat a piece of anti-royalist propaganda as Willie Hamilton could ever have dreamed up in a million years. Batty as James I must have been, he was believed (well, he was King wasn't he?), and thus cat hatred came to Britain. It was already fairly popular on the continent (God stop the Channel Tunnel – they are a barmy lot on the other side) where old women with cats were roasted alive, and the days before the Inquisition (folks with a penchant for seeking out witches and having incredibly barbaric ways of dealing with them) visited Holland, so many people had committed their cats to the deep that the canals were impassable to boats. So Britain became decidedly anti-cat and the feeling survives to this day, a relic of a crazy time when religious mania ruled (OK) and common sense fled out of the window as it usually does when religion overrides clear thinking.

Even when the madness had subsided, poor old felis domesticus still came under attack. Live cat-eating was a popular spectacle at fairs – if the right lunatic could be found to perform the feat, and such little niceties as 'room to swing a cat' (describing a small or poky room) entered our language. Room to swing a cat – well, cats were often swung, more often than not, in bags of fresh hot soot, and once the sack had burst the hapless moggy beaten to death with clubs. The sound of a cat dying in agony would melt the soul of even Sprenger and Kramer, though it had to be admitted they became pretty immune to human screams and roars of unbearable agony, but idiots have always abounded in Britain and cats were tortured, blinded and butchered.

Hang on, let's not go overboard by vilifying the British. Fun for the Hun was also provided by cats unfortunate enough to fall foul of Hessian troops stationed in Ireland, during one of the country's not too infrequent rebellions. One band of troops stationed at Kilkenny hung a pair of cats across a clothes line by their tails to watch the terrified felines rip each other apart. One trooper seeing an English officer approach, chopped off both tails and let the wretched tailless beasts escape. They explained the presence of the remaining tails by the fact that the cats had fought so savagely that only the tails remained. Hence, the term, 'fighting like Kilkenny cats', entered English usage.

Not all references to cats in our language refer to cruelty and quite a few don't even refer to cats. I'll explain that one and quickly before those not interested in things feline put the book back on the shelf. Take for instance the nursery rhyme concerning the cat and the fiddle, as unlikely a pair as ever to come together. Actually the rhyme has nothing to do with either cats or musical instruments or even cat gut, which incidentally came from sheep. It seems that one Catton, governor of Calais, was given the title 'the Faithful' by the King of France, hence Catton the Faithful. Catton le Fidele – the English could neither understand the language or pronounce the term – so Cat and the Fiddle.

Likewise, one Dick Whittington who despite the pantomine figure of bosomy young ladies dressed in male attire, was Mayor of London just before the Black Death whittled down the number of voters in his constituency, though there is no evidence he had a hint of transvestism about him. Whittington so the tale goes, travels to London, goes abroad to a country where the Moors were plagued with rats. Whittington's cat sets about them – the rats not the Moors – with a vengeance and the grateful Moors give Whittington a fortune for the beast. The truth or explanation of the legend is not quite as picturesque. Whittington became Mayor of London by dint of amassing a great fortune by fetching coal from Newcastle aboard Norwegian-built vessels called Cats – the black faces of the coal heavers giving rise to the legend of the Moors. Incidentally, don't forget North Africa was the home of the domestic cat anyway. Hey ho, we're a curious race with a curious language.

'And that was how Rupert (a black surly brute quite unlike the red-jacketed bear of the same name) came to live here, Mr er Palmer.' I was nodding visibly and my lack of interest in cats, however curious, had become apparent.

I slept that night clean and odour-free in the whiter than white sheets of Mrs Richardson, bed and breakfast purveyor, and 'catophile' – a million miles from Mars Bars, McEwan's Bitter and people with irregular bowel movements. Morning saw me saying goodbye to the lady and her houseful of cats, waking Jamie to push start the van before his usual mixed breakfast and heading north, away from picture-postcard Ullapool, along a lunar landscape to Durness.

WHIPPET-LURCHER

—8—

Der Mollonies is Daft, Every One of Dem

TSCHIFFELEY, A CURIOUS sort of bloke by any standards with even more curious interests, once decided to ride a pair of Patagonian ponies along the spine of the continent of America, called respectively the Andes and the Rocky Mountains, to illustrate the toughness of the ponies. (I say curious because I confess, I'm a bit afraid of horses.) A harmless pastime that hurt no one (though the ponies might think differently). As he approached a wild and desolate region called Bolivia in the midst of God-forsaken countryside, more bleak and forbidding than the landscape of Hell, he met a band of European gypsies en route visiting relatives. Gypsies, it seems, like water, seemingly get anywhere.

Still while travelling along a bleak inhospitable stretch of road in the west of Scotland, on a tract of land which must be the least populated area of Britain and possibly Europe, it is astonishing to meet a family of Irish tinkers and I suppose it now behoves me to elaborate the difference between tinkers and gypsies. (I've already made light reference to the subject.) It is custom I suppose to refer to any itinerant who is not overtly obnoxious, offensive and criminal as a gypsy, and if the said person does not qualify for the above mentioned titles, to label him a tinker. It is custom. It is also terribly inaccurate. I've met some really likeable and relatively straight (there is always a tendency for itinerants to sneak the odd buck or so if given half a chance) gypsies and tinkers. I've also met blacker than black versions of both men and women who seem inspired by a venomous hatred of all folk, itinerant and settled, and if Marx was correct about all property being theft, then they were hell-bent on correcting the wrongs materialistic society had wrought. They were truly, in Walsall parlance, 'A-thieves', they only stole objects beginning with 'A' – a car, a tyre, a gallon of petrol, or whatever. There's good and bad in every community I suppose, and I've known some rather devious people who weren't itinerant and did in fact live out their days in rather ritzy houses.

Gypsies, so the majority of ethnologists – a curious word for a curious group of people – believe, originated in northern India and their language called Romany is very similar to Hindi. They are called gypsies so the tale goes because when in 1407 they visited Paris, they looked so amazingly different that they cashed in on their originality by telling the credulous population that they were really Earls of Little Egypt (wherever that may be, and even the returning French crusaders were a little baffled). So Egyptian, which is how Shakespeare referred to the bands, degenerated into gypsy. Scotland had its share of gypsy-orientated problems – its share and a bit more besides. James V of Scotland believed they were top-rate entertainers, jugglers, beast trainers (they kept dancing bears trained by questionable methods) *etc*, as well as having magical powers and thus he encouraged them to his court. He learned his lesson one day when he found they were not only entertainers and had 'taking ways' so to speak, but were less entertaining thieves, rogues and pickpockets, and had very taking ways indeed. In next to no time he wanted them not only off stage, but also out of the country, and the rest of Europe followed suit in a matter of fifty or so years. Most Scottish gypsies were banished to Norway (God knows what the Norwegians had done to deserve this, maybe they had a reputation for tolerance), though the majority simply slipped south to England and established Doone-like families in Rothbury and other remote districts. As late as 1800 they were left alone by the English law, providing their offences didn't include outsiders, held their own courts and meted out their own often grisly punishment. Sadly they often dished out like punishment to outsiders (gorgios in Romany parlance), and castrating and maiming was often inflicted on anyone daft enough to violate or molest a Romany woman. Come to think of it, Mam always did warn me not to go near those 'old gypsy girls'.

Tinkers are a different ball game. Most books on itinerants indicate that tinkers are a fairly recent breed of itinerant though they bob up in folk music, often enough as seducers, rakes and a bit worse. Recent research has shown that they could be remnants of very old Celtic families who made their money not only mending pots and pans (we've come to accept a throw-away society only in recent years), but also forging swords. Nearly all the famous swords of legendary super heroes were forged by outcast people and folk with hocus-pocus powers. Later bands of itinerants made unemployed by the fact that landowners found it profitable to let arable land return to sheep pasture, swelled the number of true tinkers and after 1841 the Irish Potato Famine made hundreds of semi-itinerant Irish families up-sticks and move to America, England or anywhere. This last group of semi-itinerants were the ones Mayhew, who wrote *London Labour, London Poor*, confused with other Celtic races who had settled in London, for Mayhew states that Shelta (a bastard Gaelic language) was the most common dialect of the slums. In point of fact Mayhew spoke no Celtic language, so any foreign tongue was immediately labelled Shelta by him. He made a lot of other mistakes as well, if we are going in for nit-picking. Be that as it may, by the early nineteen hundreds the Irish tinker had come into rather hostile contact with the gypsy, particularly around the Welsh Marches and, despite the track record of the Romany as bare-knuckle battlers, the Irish tinker with his blind ferocity often came off best. A few friends of mine, Romanies and tinkers alike state, or rather swear to the fact, that after a very fierce brawl the Irish tinkers dispose of their dead without recourse to British justice. Gypsies held courts of their own, some still do, but the tinker has a justly earned reputation for lawlessness, but having said that, I must confess some of the most kind, generous and fascinating people I have met have been Irish tinkers.

'Pull up, pull up,' Jamie almost shouted. 'Dey are dem Mollonies. Dey're all mad, the Mollonies, every scat one of dem'.

Though I found Jamie tended to exaggerate, in the case of the Mollonies I found him to be fairly accurate. We pulled up alongside a medium-sized, once heavily chromed, now badly corroded caravan which disgorged an amazing number of almost identical people. All were burly, girls, boys, men, women alike, and all sported an amazing crop of carrot-coloured hair.

Both mother and father of the band were also ginger and according to Jamie were closely related as most tinker man and wife teams seem to be. Jamie explained that this was largely because no one else would marry a Mollonie, but the chances were that the majority of tinkers only meet, at least socially, people of their own persuasion, and this rather than any desire to behave incestuously, has given rise to an inbreeding programme which produces an amazingly level crop of children, bred obviously for physique rather than looks. Whereas both boys and girls had a troll-like look, a glance at the shoulders and arms of either sex indicated that they were far from stunted in growth and further still from being sickly, even the girls looked as though they were people to avoid in a brawl. All had the uncombed-look and the red, untidy hair sprouted in various directions, growing without heed to gravity or grooming.

Each member of the band apparently knew Jamie well, for as my vehicle pulled up a selection of hostile identicals raced across to the van, but on seeing Jamie as my passenger, they greeted him cordially, or perhaps on reflection not so cordially.

'How's tings in the caves, Jamie?'

'In the caves?' repeated the youngest Mollonie a grin cutting her face from ear to ear.

'Bastards,' hissed Jamie, though not too loudly I noticed.

The recipient of his comments was a powerfully built nine-year-old. What troubled me most was the interest the group paid to my lurchers.

'Whippet/greyhounds, are they?' the identicals shouted, and though I denied their supposed sight hound lineage, the youth continued with his whippet/greyhound spiels in terms which amounted to eulogy on the merits of the hybrid.

'I had a dog when I was a boy,' (he was scarcely more than twenty) 'a whippet/greyhound like dose,' he gestured at Fathom and Penguin and I sensed the futility of repeating their breeding. 'Dat dog', he mused pensively, shaking his head in a gesture of nostalgia, 'was taking' – he assessed an implausible figure – '75, no, 80 hares a night – by himself,' he put in for good measure. He paused, I sensed he was giving a little thought to the next far-fetched tale. 'At Appleby Fair,' – the Mecca for itinerants – 'dat dog – I was offered £10 000 for him and would I sell? No sir, I would not. Nothin', no, nothin', could make me part with dat dog – a whippet/greyhound,' he put in for good measure, 'like dose.'

I warmed to him, the only itinerant I've ever met who refused to be separated from his beloved dog.

'Yes, yes,' he added, to cap the tale, after much pensive head-shaking and nostalgia.

'What happened to him?' I questioned, wondering what had become of this, the beau ideal of all lurchers.

He snapped out of his reverie.

'Er, I swopped him for a borzy [borzoi] wid a great big long 'ed – a strange dog that,' he muttered ambling off towards a caravan which again disgorged an impossible number of children.

Another red-haired youth circled the van.

'Jamie,' I hissed, 'they're going to steal these dogs.'

'No', hissed Jamie. 'They'll try to buy them, and you'll get pissed off with offers to swop them, but they'll no' steal them from ye,' and no sooner had he spoken than the lad started negotiating a transaction.

'Will you sell them, Mister? Sell them?'

He produced a wad of notes to prove his offer. I shook my head.

'Will you swap dem for a . . .' he thought up a suitable pedigree, 'a whippet/greyhound?'

He raced towards the truck and produced a very dirty-coated dog, vaguely brindled with a slightly rough coat, 'A whippet/greyhound,' he added.

Again I shook my head.

'Will you swap him for a stag hound/greyhound?'

Again he raced towards the van materialising with the selfsame dog, the same coat, the same oil stains.

'He'll do this all day,' Jamie spat out. 'They're mad, all the Mollonies.'

Old Pat, the father of the band, ambled towards the van – a slightly more lined and ragged edition of the children. He twanged the braces holding up his trousers across his prominent bloated gut.

'Don' know if I want you here, Jamie, not after what your brother did wid the brass horse. The bastard,' he spat out with hatred.

I just had to enquire about the brass horse! Apparently when they were camped near Penrith, Old Pat Mollonie owned a brass horse, his pride and joy, an ornament much admired by his fellow tinkers to whom Pat showed the heavy brass object incessantly, at every opportunity in fact. Jamie's brother had sensed its value to the old man and popped into the caravan and took it. He had then offered to sell Pat the horse to make a pair. Pat didn't believe his good luck at the acquisition of an exact replica of his beloved ornament and had paid up without a haggle, a handsome price well beyond the value of the ornament. McPhee was miles away before Pat realised the deception. Glancing at the scarred and battered face of Old Pat, and noting the immense arms as ginger-haired and powerful as the legs of a Tamworth pig, I couldn't but wonder at the fate of Jamie's brother when Old Pat caught up with him.

'I ain't a forgivin' sort, Jamie, tell him dat, Jamie, tell him dat. I ain't a forgivin' sort. I'll find him.' He made a twisting action with his hands and I winced.

We left the van as the old man waved us towards his wagon.

'Yer'll hev tea,' he more or less commanded, and his wife, a ginger-haired, hairy-armed woman poured tea into delicately made bone china. 'I ain't forgot the horse, mind you, Jamie. Ain't forgot.'

A gingery son raced across to us with a huge old-fashioned brass-knobbed bedstead of the sort that Chelsea antique dealers offer to clientelle. The old man noticed the condition of the purchase and patted the lad on the head.

'Must be worth £15,' he speculated carefully as an art connoisseur examining a Rembrandt. 'How much did yer pay for it?'

'£20,' came the answer.

The pat changed to a backhander that spun the boy and bedstead away from the wagon.

Pat's wife broke into the conversation, which was uncommon, for Romany and tinker women are a little careful about interrupting the conversation of their menfolk.

'I knew Jamie's grandmother when she lived in der caves at Staxigoe,' she trilled, as though she was name dropping.

'Liar,' whispered Jamie.

'What was dat?' demanded Pat.

'Where's the fire?' answered Jamie, rubbing his hands as if cold, and ambled towards a pile of wood, rubber tyres and rubbish which belched out heat and filth into the black faces of the children.

'His granny did live there, in der caves,' went on the hairy-armed woman. 'When it was a high tide the people dat lived nearby had to pull 'em up de cliffs wid ropes and they'd dunk 'em in the water cos they was stealing things,' she put in 'Ain't got no time for thieves.'

'Like his brudder,' said Old Pat, venomously, still sore about the horse trick. 'His grandad were straight though,' he added, rather generously, giving virtue to the horse thief's pedigree.

'Where are you heading?' I said, trying to make conversation, feeling rather inadequate, certainly physically inadequate amongst such a band.

'Aberdeen for de tatty picking,' Pat replied, twanging his braces which gave a resounding thump against his prominent gut.

I drew a map of the country in my mind and said 'Aberdeen is due east from here. From where have you come?'

'Inverness,' Pat replied, twanging his braces yet once more leaving me in more of a geographical muddle than ever.

Seemingly itinerants in general, and tinkers in particular, wander where and when they will with no sense of purpose and no time schedule. A commendable sort of life to those who enjoy it and about as mentally untaxing an existence as anyone could imagine. Gypsies, according to Moses, a friend of mine who is a settled gypsy, live according to a fairly rigid timetable. They never seem to have calendars in their wagons and yet any gypsy can tell you the date and day of the week without thinking about it. Most of their lives seems to be regulated by the times of the fairs. Appleby – a summer solstice fair – seems to be the highlight or focal point of the calendar, with Barnaby Fair acting as a sort of precursor to the main event. Horse fairs in Gloucester seem to punctuate the year and various other fairs throughout the country seem to be other events which regulate the itinerant body clocks. Few are able to read sign posts yet all arrived on time at Appleby. Fewer still are in possession of a diary of events yet all arrive on schedule at places of importance. How Scottish tinkers, called blackfaced tinkers by Vesey Fitzgerald who not only travelled with them but had their confidence, measure out the year is a bit baffling as fairs are few and far between in Scotland, but they cross the border on time for Appleby in much the same way perhaps that swallows move south on time, on course, despite spells of Indian summers or wintery autumns.

An amazing number of people seemed to fill the campsite, all seemingly alike and all disgorged from three caravans. Mrs Mollonie, wife of Old Pat, and brood mare without equal, presided over the entire flock, and I was struck by the once popular but dismally futile exercise concerning how many people could be piled into a Mini (Austin/ Morris/Cooper). Night times must have involved similar exercises in bedtime ingenuity in the Mollonie's wagons. It is often said that tinkers live according to their own rules and regulations and are not in any way influenced by the laws of the kerengro (Romany for people who live in houses) and perhaps this is so. They certainly don't go running to the police for crimes like theft, rape and even murder, and deal with such offenders discreetly or perhaps not so discreetly in their own particular way. Sampson, the gypsiologist – an incongruous title, for Sampson was an authority not only on gypsies but on the itinerant bands wandering Great Britain and swarming over from southern Ireland – believed that whereas Romanies have fairly strict codes of conduct within their own group (anything seems to go where us gorgios are concerned), tinkers do not have such rules and taboos to govern their ways of life. Sampson was a bit prejudiced about tinkers – he once had an unnerving experience with one in Liverpool while he was making notes on the language they were speaking – but any group living so tightly together must be bound by not only a rough and ready guideline to life but by strict rules. Incest is rare, possibly because of the dreadful rewards such a crime reaps when the girl's family are alerted to the problem, but so is theft within the family. Communal property is to some extent practised, much as amongst the Eskimos, but whereas the first up within the wagons is invariably the best dressed, personal property – such as Old Pat's horse is respected and held almost sacred.

What is fascinating, however, is that itinerants – be they gypsies or Romanies – are seldom stuck for something to do at night. True, when near a town or village, they swarm into pubs and cafés often making pests of themselves, but now, camped miles from anywhere on a stretch of lonely road twixt Ullapool and Durness, they set to with a vengeance to entertain themselves.

The second wave of children, or perhaps a few of the original batch – it was impossible to tell – congregated around the steamy windows of my van to view the 'whippet/greyhounds', each and every one, boy and girl alike, coming across to relate outlandish tales of the prowess of their own whippet/greyhound, and to make me offers for my own lurchers.

However, just before evening drew on I had just the faintest premonition that matters were about to turn a little ugly and the fact that

Jamie had somehow disappeared from the site did nothing but confirm my worst fears. I think matters began to warm up when Pat gathered the group around the fireside to tell a tale.

'Now der best, no der very best bare-knuckle fighter I ever met' – shouts of Flynn, O'Flaherty and Tuggy (whoever they might be) were stopped by the shaking of Old Pat's head – 'was', he went on, 'Big Ezzie the tinker.'

Now curious as it might appear I knew Big Ezzie the tinker, or at least an Ezzie the tinker, so my ears pricked up at the mention of the name. The Ezzie I knew, he might have been the same, was a much-scarred middle-aged man renowned for his strength and pugilistic prowess. Old Pat had sensed my interest and had quickened the tale.

'Big Ezzie next to Phil Connors' (everyone nodded, I out of respect – I hadn't a clue who he was) 'was the fightinest man der ever was. At Appleby' – everything, according to Pat at least, happened at Appleby and from my knowledge of the place gleaned from three visits, just about everything did happen there – 'Ezzie was fightin a man called McKie Clore'.

'Why was they fightin?' put in Patricia, a thirteen-year-old with a physique like Mohammed Ali, a damsel more likely to inflict GBH than encounter distress.

'Dey was fightin, just because threy was fightin.' Pat quelled her interest in a flash with an impatient wave of the hand. 'Big Ezzie must have taken fifty or maybe more blows to the face and not caught McKie at all for McKie could dance out of der way.' Old Pat gave an incongruous imitation of this Appleby Daniel Mendoza, protruding gut bulging against braces, 'But Ezzie was just waiting, and quick as a flash he smashes McKie with a blow.' He dealt son Donnie a massive swipe which felled the eighteen-year-old but scarcely noticing or waiting to see if the youth had been damaged by the jaw-cracking imitation of Ezzie's coup de grace, he continued, 'At Appleby next year he knocked out a horse with his fist – jes for a bet, hitting it in der face as it ran at 'im'.

Four or five youngsters twixt nine and maybe twelve, boy and girl alike, inflamed by the account of this formidable Ezzie were on their feet battling, each one imitating the gypsy folk hero in the same way that youths of my own age sought to be famous football stars and I was about to grin at the spectacle when a large grimy paw touched me on the shoulder and turning round I came face to face with Eddie, the oldest (or maybe not) son of Old Pat.

'Will you fight me?' he asked, without aggression or rancour, in the same way as a friend might ask to borrow a car or a garden hose.

'Christ, no,' I replied, gazing at the ham-like muscles with horror.

'Why?' he asked, apparently hurt by my refusal, 'Have I said somethink to upset you?'

'No, no, not a bit,' I stuttered, feeling the malaise of childhood returning once again, accompanied by a cold nauseous sweat, I must add.

'Fight someone who wants to fight you, Eddie,' shouted Old Pat, slamming the youngster with a punch to the head.

Donnie who had recovered from the slapstick attack of his father's imitation of Ezzie's mighty blow, immediately stripped to the waist and the pair set to with a vengeance, the rest of the band shouting encouragement to the brothers.

After watching the opponents for just a matter of a few seconds, I was grateful that no temporary madness had tempted me to accept Eddie's kind offer to fight him. Neither Eddie nor Donnie had any form of fighting style, but the windmill-like blows were delivered hard, fast and with crushing force, primarily in the way that small boys fight, to the head and to the face and in next to no time the pair were daubed in blood which flowed copiously from nose and mouth wounds. I watched fascinated yet horrified as they pounded each other to a bloody pulp just for the hell of it, for no prize or matter of honour, and took to wondering if the bare-knuckle fighters of old were a different breed of man from the ones we know today. Were Sayers and Heenan, matched for world title honours in the mid-1800s, and who battled for some four hours until Heenan was blind and Sayers had one arm hanging limply at his side, more than human or because of the brutalising effect of such conflicts, less than human? As I watched these two troll-like wretches battle it out in the dying hours of the day, the savage scene lit by the lights of camp fires I realised that there was little honour and no dignity in the bare-knuckle or leather Cestus battle fought between Odysseus and Ajax, or the grudge contests fought between Humphries and my own hero Daniel Mendoza, the battling Jew of Cheapside. As the faces of the antagonists became bloodier and more bruised by the minute, I became aware that the gloved contests twixt trained and medically examined opponents bore no resemblance to the fist-to-face battlers who smashed, crushed and mutilated each other a century ago to please a powdered effete and often effeminate audience. Finally Donnie shouted, 'Adit', and the pair stopped battling, various members of the family touching the battered features of their favourites and daubing their champion's blood on their own brows. I had seen such spectacles at Appleby and sadly they were battles of this sort which were to bring the end of respectable shows such as Lambourn and had wondered the origins of such barbarous rituals. I looked around at the faces of the Mollonies. I felt aware they would be unlikely to be able to shed light on the subject of fistic rituals or folk legends of any sort unless they included Big Ezzie. I think I may have shaken my head in disbelief but the action must have attracted the bloodied and unbowed Eddie who strode across to me.

'Der yer want to sell dem . . . [I waited] whippet/greyhounds?' he asked, through swollen lips.

I shook my head in answer and he shuffled off to live again various highlights of the fight with members of his family gesticulating widely, emulating his best and cruellest blows to his brother. Funnily enough, just before the band folded or interlocked themselves into the cramped trailers Jamie appeared clutching a half-empty can of McEwan's.

We, Jamie and I, slept in the van that night and I dreamed dreams of puny and ill-informed do-gooders who sought to protect ferocious and formidable people such as the Mollonies from the corrupting and ostracising world of suburban respectability. In a TV speeded-up type composite, I dreamed of Old Pat like a Titan swallowing whole Donnie and Eddie and chomping through the muscular Patricia for afters. I awoke at dawn, released the dogs for a few minutes to 'exercise' themselves for the want of a better word, carefully watching them I must add, and prepared to leave.

Donnie appeared, face swollen like a long-fought pit bull terrier.

'What are dem lurchers in the back of der van?' he asked yet again.

I stared hard at him, the lad who had asked the same question a dozen times the day before.

'Whippet/greyhounds,' I said slowly and deliberately.

'Aw, they're no good, no good at all. Me Dad wouldn't let us have a whippet/greyhound on de wagons.'

Yes, Jamie could be correct, the Mollonies is mad, all mad.

BEARDY —

—9—

Bearded Collies and Bedlam

I WAS 'DRIVEN IN', as Jamie put it, rather disparagingly I thought, twixt Durness and Tongue, two small villages masquerading as towns, at least on the map, which lie in coves along the most northernly and bleak coast of mainland Britain. I suppose my capitulation to the rigours of the elements and my own body filth, had started the day before on the westerly road between the Mollonies and Durness. My van had started clanging loudly and finally juddered to a halt. It had failed to respond to the loving drop-kick lavished on the side of the bonnet, which worked as a rule, and in despair I was forced to phone the ever-patient and much-maligned (see chapter 1) RAC.

Now, the RAC and I suppose the AA for that matter have very few I-thank-you-sir, touch-the-cap obligatory smile (or in my case look of disgusted bewilderment) patrol men in the extreme north, which so the geography department of the school tells me, is the least populated coast in Britain, and a visit will tell the reader why. Hence the RAC usually appoint a general factotum from a local garage. In my case this turned out to be a tiny elfin-like man who spoke in a dialect which wasn't only not understood by me, but also left Jamie looking a bit bewildered.

After about five minutes under the bonnet the elfin mechanic gave a sharp intake of breath, raised himself on the balls of his feet and said very slowly and ominously, 'Are you going far?'

'Birmingham,' I replied, for no one, but no one in northern Scotland has even heard of Lichfield.

'Ah,' he replied, and threw in another 'Ah' for good measure before diving under the bonnet again.

In minutes and a few turns of the ignition the van was juddering, vibrating and clanging again and we set off for Durness, a tiny port which hosts a ferry to the uninhabited peninsular Cape Wrath. An eagle or a giant buzzard flapped upwards from a road-casualty rabbit splattered on the highway.

'What the hell was that, Jamie?' I yelled excitedly, jabbing him with my elbow.

'A big bird,' he replied yawning.

'What sort?' I asked, irritated by his blasé indifference.

'A bloody big bird,' he added for good measure.

I shook my head at his indifference to ornithology, and felt a little smug about my own, thereby making the error of underestimating him. Within minutes I knew the mistake I had made.

We turned a sharp bend on the road and a grey, blue and white gull hobbled across the highway. I stepped out of the car to examine the damaged bird.

'Dinna do that,' Jamie warned. 'They gob.'

But of course I knew better. The gull turned and shot a filthy cod-liver-oil-yellow fluid into my face, hair and clothes, before fluttering off. The stench clung to my hair, my clothes, my skin and even Jamie wrinkled his nose in disgust.

'Them's fulmars,' he spat out. 'They allus do that. Gob – just like I said they would. The wind up here drops them a bit, knocks the go out of them. Two days rest and they are up again – if cats and such like don't get 'em.' he added indifferently.

I tried in vain to remove the smell of the fishy oil, but still reeked of it when we pulled into the park of the tiny café in Durness.

The café was almost empty apart from one jocular Geordie who joined us as soon as we sat down.

'Hey, bonny lad' – the traditional Geordie greeting – 'it's nice to meet someone from home,' he muttered, meaning England I suppose. The Geordie continued telling us how he did a country and western act (West Hartlepool?) and was working the north coast from Wick down to Ullapool. I mentioned we were going in the opposite direction and he shook his head. 'It's bleak out there for nine months of the year, the weather's bad and for the other three it's bloody awful. Have you tipped cod liver oil on your clothes?' he asked, sniffing the air for the tell-tale scent of my indiscretion with the fulmar.

I explained but Jamie remained silent, only half-heartedly listening to the conversation. We walked back to the van leaving the Geordie to his lonely cowboy-booted Texan-hatted exile.

'From which country was he?' asked Jamie.

I stopped and stared at him. The accent in Newcastle is a bit difficult to understand perhaps, but the thought of a Geordie-accented country and western singer singing to an audience who were wondering how far west 'western' meant and which country 'country' meant, sprang to mind.

'Newcastle,' I replied.

'Was he an Atomic?' Jamie asked.

'What the hell is an Atomic?' I questioned, as I'd heard him use the expression before.

'Them that come up here to work at Dounreay [an atomic energy plant]. White settlers who come up here to take our jobs. To take over our jobs!!' I closed my eyes and saw a white-coated Dr McPhee triggering off the odd China Syndrome or so out of sheer pique that someone had left the lid off his McEwan's can or bitten into his Mars Bar.

'Would you like to be an Atomic, Jamie?'

'I would not,' he shook his head vigorously to reinforce the denial. 'The bastards get kids with two heads. The papers don't tell you about it cos the hospital doctors are made to smother 'em soon as they're born.'

He went on to relate more horrors which seemingly go hand in hand with being an Atomic, macabre stories of men and women having a full-time Ready Brek glow and mutations enough to make the Fantastic Four seem credible. According to Jamie, the sea around Dounreay shone with an incandescent glow at night and people who lived near had to obey a curfew lest they should see the luminous sea and leak the tale of the radioactive sea coast to the press.

'That's all that's at Thurso,' he ended his spiel, 'that and the spies.' (The spies turned out to be the staff of the American Tracking Base close by Thurso, each one of which according to Jamie was a Burgess/McClean figure or a Mata Hari type, depending on their sexes.)

'Sounds a hairy sort of place, Thurso,' I mused, sniggering as we slammed the van doors.

'Boring actually,' Jamie replied. 'Sod all going on there, 'cept the Atomics, and I've heard they can infect you.'

However, after two days dirt and a splodge of fulmar vomit staining my clothes, long before we reached Tongue – an anti-Bonnie Prince Charlie town where everyone seemed to be called McKay – I decided to go in and not only bath, but sleep in a clean bed free of the scent of Jamie, lurchers and the defence mechanisms of fulmars. Bed and breakfast houses are thick on the ground along the coast and the further east we went the more numerous the B/B signs. I told Jamie of my intentions and he sucked his teeth in disgust at my weakness.

'Yer bathed only two days ago. My uncle used to bath regularly every week,' he sneered. 'It weakened him dreadfully and he died of cancer, I think it was,' he speculated.

Anyway, braving the possible carcinogenous problems resulting from bathing and clean bedclothes I might encounter, I booked into one of the houses leaving Jamie to sleep in the van which I parked on the side of the main road, after first removing the key, I must add.

The house was immaculate and owned by a very hospitable retired shepherd and his wife who had been born on the North Coast, but had gone to tend sheep in Perthshire when the jobless 1920s had caused the population of the Highlands to shrink dramatically. The house was a fascinating glimpse into the past and the walls were literally covered with sepia-tinted photographs of a bygone age which made one realise that the twentieth century arrived in the Highlands with a disturbing and not a particularly welcome explosion. In 1873 Frank Buckland the world famous eccentric and gourmet had come to John O' Groats on an exploratory trip sponsored by the Ministry of Agriculture and Fisheries and had commented on how Caithness was an island where time had stood still and Mr McCleod, the retired shepherd, had seemingly made it his life's work to collect regalias of ways of life during those pre-Buckland years. An anachronism, a man more at home a century before his birth, just about described him and whereas the typical Highlander has often a justly earned reputation for being dour, the very fact that someone showed an interest in his collection of ghosts long past encouraged him to relate fascinating tales.

Inventions seem to arrive at just about the right time to suit the course of civilisation. Erlich's 606 was discovered by intention or accident at the time when syphilis was becoming so common as to make any innocent shy of using a public toilet, let alone of becoming promiscuous. Ross came up with the answer to malaria in 1902, giving the powers that be about thirteen years to work on controlling the disease before conducting a military campaign in the mosquito-infested Middle East (it wasn't all Lawrence of Arabia stuff). Likewise the camera was invented just in time to record the sterner, less romantic side of the American Civil War. Improved photographic techniques allowed those with an artistic flair, opportunity to go out and put a fast-changing world on film slide before the inexorable roll of all mod cons, radio, TV and Cecil B. DeMille type epics completely replaced simple living, bucket under board toilets, spring water and village hall magic lantern slides. Photographers flocked to the north to film the land where time stood still, or was just about to change. As a result of photography, the people invading the land brought hitherto an unknown if temporary prosperity to a land with Third World standards and gentle curious Third World ideology and expectations. In doing so, however, the tourists hastened the change, precipitated the metamorphosis for the good or the bad, is still being disputed.

Sexual equality, a present day term, was the order of the day at the turn of the 1880s. Women worked alongside men in the fields, mucking the land with cartloads of rotting seaweed, living on a diet of mutton, potatoes and fish, carrying men pickaback fashion to the fishing boats, their long skirts awash with saltwater lest their men soaked the insides of their seaboots, and finally dying alongside these selfsame men when both were prematurely worn out by an all too inclement and rigorous life. Hard times, but there was sexual equality, real sexual equality, if only because the life was so hard that there was little time for sexual role playing and little leisure to compare how hard the lot of either sex was. Both sire and dam played their parts in the hard and hectic game called life, and for some reason procreated hordes of children who would continue their back-breaking, physically destructive mode of life for yet another generation. Tuberculosis, called consumption in those days, ever present pneumonia, bronchitis (for the climate is damp and conducive to such diseases), and from time to time cholera destroyed men and women alike and photographs indicate that the aging process was accelerated by such a life, but sexual equality women had, if only because they shared and partook of the hardships and endured a less than desirable lifestyle alongside their men folk. What is called sexual equality today is different, not only in its social form but in its texture and physical analysis. Today's sexually liberated woman follows an equally predictable way of life, as predictable as that of the Highland woman of old and perhaps in the long run less satisfying though perhaps more soul-destroying. Anne, a once, or better still, twice-married woman with 2.4 kids, a husband, and an obligatory mortgage decides she is not getting what she wants out of life (she is incidentally not quite sure what she wants), and that her nine-to-five husband is getting a better deal out of his life. True, he will probably die of a coronary or develop ulcers as a result of his equally monotonous lifestyle and pop off to the great singles club in the sky long before his dearly beloved, but to Anne, disenchanted and on the way to becoming liberated, hubby is seemingly getting a better deal. She will invent a whole host of complaints to justify her leaving and become venomous at the thought of yet another further spell of incarceration euphemistically called 'marriage', and hey ho she is living by herself again – well, at least as by herself as 2.4 children will allow her to be. In no time flat she will be taking magazines, reading articles by those out to protect and encourage black lesbian unmarried mothers with damp houses and a drug addiction problem, and well on the way to a temporary rejection, a very temporary rejection, of making herself attractive to men. The metamorphosis accelerates with Anne developing her interests, taking an OU course in sociology, enjoying a short-lived spate of bed-leaping with a variety of very unsuitable equally bored OU beaus before becoming even more disenchanted, even more viper-tongued about men in general, and her now happily remarried husband in particular. Liberated? Well, maybe. Biologically aberrant, unproductive certainly, unloved, unlovely invariably and sexually equal certainly, for there are male equivalents aplenty in this chop and change, alimony-orientated 'I'll not let him get custody of the children' unhappy world, which makes me get down on my knees and thank God for my bachelor status. And now gazing at the sepia tints of women long past, careworn, weather-worn, staying alongside their men in sickness and in health, ignorant of decree nisis and absolutes, I cannot help but think that Germaine Greer's book on the development of the modern woman should be subtitled 'Ladies, You have nothing to gain but your chains'. There in the living room of one James McCleod, retired shepherd, the photographs presented a way of life more taxing perhaps, but more spiritually rewarding than the solo club bed-hopping world of the Midlands I had just left behind. I snapped out of my reverie and ceased staring at the browning photographs.

Behind McCleod's chair two elderly bearded collies peered at me, both as work-worn, both as aged by wind and weather as McCleod himself. I asked him about them for bearded collies are rare now that the ubiquitous border collie has come north into the Highlands. McCleod thought a moment before replying, an admirable trait in a man, though one which is becoming rarer by the year. 'I suppose', he began, 'I keep them because they have served me well, and I keep beardies rather than borders because my father did so, and his father before him, for they also served them well, and because', he added, 'it is a Scottish breed and I am a Scot.'

Yet despite the fact that the bearded collie is regarded as being as Scottish as Rob Roy himself, there is a tale that the breed is not even British let alone Scottish. By 1500 Europe had begun to realise that Scotland existed and was not just a hostile appendage stuck on top of England, and trade was starting to flourish between the Scots and the rest of the Hanseatic League. A Polish trader called Kazmiez Grabski had left Gdansk to trade grain for wool in Scotland and had purchased a herd of black-faced sheep to ship home to Poland. The shepherds were however unable to get their native collies, probably precursors of border collies, to drive the difficult sheep up the gangplank of the rocking boat, and confusion reigned. Grabski then produced a very hirsute type of herding dog which harried, nipped and bit the sheep until they were only too glad to get aboard, whereupon Grabski traded the dogs, two bitches and a dog, for a matched black-faced ewe and ram. The tale is almost certainly apocryphal, but then a very special breed of dog is required to herd black-faced sheep, for black-faced are a very special sort of sheep.

Forget the silly sheep of the Downs as big as calves and docile as hearth cats. Black-face sheep are not of this species. Early records written by monks more akin to Mendel than the Venerable Bede make reference to sheep so fierce that they could deter the attentions of wolves let alone marauding dogs – and it requires a rather special breed of dog to face the wool-covered head of bone and convoluted horn. As a child I had seen a sheep-worrying bull terrier, a white English bull terrier, still an unspoilt canine gladiator in my youth, given a last chance to repent its ways by being locked in a shed with a black-faced ram. The cacophony of barking and grunting had been terrible and the owner had come away lest he relented and took the dog out of the shed, and allowed it to continue its sheep-worrying ways. An hour later he had returned to find a very bloody, badly bitten, earless, tailless ram, whose body was covered in hideous lacerations and a very dead pulverised bull terrier. The ram was still dealing butt after ferocious butt, at the very dead dog. It needs a very game dog to herd such rams.

Rams! Even the ewes are cast in bronze. In 1948 the climate of Britain hiccupped and a winter never to be forgotten blitzed the land from north to south, no one escaping the icy blast and deep snows. Mam attributed the winter to the effects of the Hiroshima A-bomb but then she attributed the death of her Busy Lizzie to the selfsame blast. My sister gave birth to my niece in that year and I floundered three miles to fetch a doctor to attend my sister. I needed the doctor myself by the time I arrived at the surgery, for I was half-dead with exposure even though snow ploughs cleared the valley roads four or five times a day until the telephone poles were all but covered with snow. *Pathe News*, our only visual contact with the outside world, had a field day, helicopters filming dying farm animals from the Highlands to Cornwall, and Scotland had more than its share of hard weather. The snows melted and revealed sheep – some dead admittedly, for they had been buried in drifts for nearly a month, but many survived, and though they were emaciated walked away to live and breed another generation. Curiously spring saw a very large crop of lambs, for, perhaps like groundsel, black-faced sheep threatened with extinction breed with great vigour to prevent cessation of the type.

Bearded collies were once common in the Highlands, now they are rare and working strains as uncommon as hen's teeth. Now border collies are found on most farms, narrow-faced less colourful in type, but with an earnestness of purpose which is hard to fault. Shepherds claim that the bearded collie was apt to 'ball up' in deep snow or mud – to become so caked in mire and so sodden with rain as to be a misery to the shepherd and itself. The chances are, however, that the now popular sheepdog trials brought about the loss of popularity of the breed for the trials require a clockwork precision and above all a silent dog, for a single bark brings about the disqualification of the collie. Bearded collies were bred to range wide and to control large and fierce flocks. They used not only their teeth to attack and drive their wards but barked frantically when trying to move a solid block of horn and thick-boned skull. They were not suitable for the Saturday afternoon displays of a shepherd's skills in front of admiring crowds and attentive if bewildered TV audiences who gasped in wonder at the finely honed instinct of the border collie. Hence the beardie began to trickle down the precipitous and slippery slope to extinction. True, more hirsute, more glamorous strains were gathered together by fanciers and registered with the Kennel Club and flowing-coated collies brushed and tended by loving owners are now common at many dog shows, but these are a different type from the scruffy mud-bedraggled working bearded collie, whose only grooming was to be shorn alongside the sheep at shearing time, its scruffy fleece contributing to the bulk of the wool taken from its black-faced wards. There is perhaps a respite, a brief breathing space for the working beardie, however. In recent years a form of blindness called the collie eye anomaly has smitten strains of the working border, particularly the trial strains and there is also evidence to suggest that the finely honed herding instinct of the border has become a little too finely honed for its own good. A series of freak occurrences seem to surround some types of trial bred border collies – some of the tales are a little far-fetched, others have more than a grain of truth about them. Stories of turkeys, hens, ducks, sheep and even bullocks being herded to exhaustion and death by collies who cannot control this exaggerated instinct, seem to make the papers with alarming regularity. Perhaps there is hope for the more phlegmatic, perhaps even more thinking beardie yet – but then perhaps not, for man only becomes aware of a loss of breed after he has lost it irretrievably.

McCleod fascinated me and made me feel oddly lacking in knowledge. He had been born in the year which had seen the end of the Boer War and the invention of the ominous words 'concentration camps'. The isolated farmsteads twixt Tongue and Durness really were isolated in those days but the Education Act of 1870 insisted that even children living in isolated farmsteads should be educated and if the children were unable to attend school then the school must attend the children. Teachers, dedicated as only Victorian teachers seemed to be, travelled twixt the groups of houses which dotted the hills and stayed a week at each group living with the families, sleeping in the houses and dishing out a shade more than the Three 'Rs' if McCleod was anything to go by. He knew not only the traditional and baffling poetry of Burns but a host of English poets as well, and quoted them fluently. He had a fair knowledge of Shakespeare, though he had never been to England. Geography, history and a working knowledge of science had all been taught at these 'side schools', as such places were called, by unqualified teachers like as not, but McCleod had left at 14 with education to put the best of our modern children to shame. Perhaps there is much to commend the high technology of the bigger than big comprehensive schools, and perhaps not. McCleod might have become another Einstein in such an environment, or more than likely would have degenerated to a malcontented nothing of the type I was teaching and my own particularly unproductive production line was regularly turning on to the job market.

Ironically he had returned to Durness to die, as he considered the barren Grampian mountains where he had served as a shepherd, to be a bit too crowded for him. He had as he put it, everything he needed in life and on the surface of it was the most contented man I have ever met. Out of place in time he may have been, as antiquated in his ways as the faded photographs on his wall, but he was living the life he wanted unfettered by convention, unhindered by the fast moving current of twentieth-century life. At least that was how it appeared on first glance. Only once did I notice a slight tear in his satisfied and composed attitude to life. I let slip I was a teacher, a mere accident as I am scarcely proud of the fact, no more proud in fact than is the profession of me, and immediately McCleod's wife leapt up and brought from the parlour a 1940-type photograph of a young girl. She polished the glass of the framed photograph lovingly, as my mother polished the photograph of Margaret my sister, my mother's only child for Mam had given birth to one child and two supernumeraries. 'This is our daughter Fiona.' (What else? All north west coast Scottish children are called Fiona, so it seems.) 'She too is a teacher. She teaches in the Midlands.' She cast a glance across at her husband who shuffled upstairs to fetch Fiona's letter written on school note paper. They beamed in pride at the photograph. 'We saved hard to send her to college,' they added proudly. 'We wanted something better for her, something better than living out here.' He gestured at the darkened window and the splendid rugged country beyond it, bathed in a pollution-free sea. I was about to cast a blind, bored and unseeing eye over the letter, for family matters interest me little, when I noticed the headed notepaper. To my astonishment it was from a junior school which fed the comprehensive where I was teaching. I gazed out of the window at the darkness. 'We wanted something better for her,' repeated McCleod. The school was a hell hole, a raging bedlam, a grim junior school edition of the hellish place where I was teaching, an EPA school – a school of special educational difficulties our local councillor had called it; a training ground for thieves, murderers and muggers, the less kind CID has termed it. 'We wanted something better' – Oh, Mr McCleod, you and your sepia-tinted photographs and peace of mind, you are not of this world, let alone of this time!

—10—

Goshawk for a Poor Man?

WE TRAVELLED ALONG the bleak and forbidding North Coast, made bleaker yet by the onset of winter, towards Thurso, a once prosperous fishing town that is now dying on the edge of the Pentland Firth. Strangely, Thurso was almost a magical name for a mining village boy where more people owned a pigeon loft than a bathroom and every child, boy and girl alike, knew the 'race points' north and south. Thurso was the last mainland race point north and the next race was a forbidding one hundred and fifty miles of water away at Lerwick, another almost mythical race point in the Shetlands.

Jamie opened yet another Mars Bar, the profits, no doubt, of yet another illegal 'lift' either at the café at Durness or a furtive shopping venture at one of the few shops in Durness village. Magnanimously he proffered me a bite, his long-unwashed hands clutching the bar strategically lest I should accept his offer and take too large a portion of his swag. I declined his generosity with a shake of the head. McPhee was a gastronomic miracle, either a medically baffling form of homo sapiens (only a form) which could exist on an unvaried vitamin-free diet, or living proof that mankind could shout, 'Sod the nutritionists', and exist on Mars Bars alone. Throughout four hundred miles and seven days of travelling Jamie had existed on Mars Bars, washed down with draughts of McEwan's Bitter and remained hale and hearty, if a trifle belligerent and intolerant of all other forms of humans we had met. However, a few nights of sleeping rough and non-stop travelling was playing hell with my system, leaving me exhausted, dyspeptic, irritable and ill with a dull pain across the left side of my chest. Jamie was on the other hand, despite his nauseous, frightened-weasel smelling body odour and some even less pleasant smells from other areas of his body, the perfect advertisement that 'Man shall live by Mars Bars alone' (with the occasional slurp of McEwan's), to misquote the Bible.

Perhaps there are in fact two kinds of human being living on this planet, I mused. Homo sapiens and homo-not-so-sapiens McEwanssii, a more robust, viable (though workshy) species which, providing the A-bomb blast did not destroy the brewery at Inverness and the factory at Slough, would survive the holocaust to populate the world with a race of intolerant dark-skinned savages with an alimentary system which could exist on food of dubious nutritional value and an ability to regurgitate at will if the diet was not exactly to their liking.

'What yer thinking?' Jamie broke my thread of thought. 'That's the trouble wid you, yer allus thinking – like a bleeding Atomic,' he added, with a sneer – his ultimate insult and threw in a quick and loud belch to reinforce his statement.

Funnily enough as he spoke, we were passing the atomic energy plant at Dounreay, an apparently innocuous open-plan type site without any obvious security force of the sort one sees in Matt Helm films. Jamie's face darkened still more and he grunted in anger at the sight of the workers leaving the plant on bikes, cars and vans.

'Atomics,' he snarled. 'Dirty Atomics,' he added, to reinforce his insult. 'Dey are', he made three or four attempts at the word, 'polluting, de air and dis land with mess and things,' he almost spat out in anger, treating the selfsame air to a filthy belch or so before winding down the window and vomiting on the road. 'I hate dem who spoil the country,' he added, mopping his mouth with the back of his hand, at the same time hurling a dozen or so Mars wrappers and some dented empty cans of McEwan's on to the road. 'Bastards,' he added, in contempt for those who seemed hell-bent on destroying the equilibrium of his hygenic and tidy little world.

He scratched his dark black and dirty hair madly, making me wonder that should, by the oddest quirk of fate, I chance to continue my relationship with Jamie, a crate of tick eating birds of the sort which accompany rhinoceroses might be an appropriate Christmas present for him. It was Jamie, however, who decided to discontinue the relationship.

'I got relatives, relations like in Thurso,' he snorted as we passed a sign which said Scrabster. 'Drop us in Thurso will ya? Drop us at the Glebe [a piece of land once belonging to the Church]. I'll show you where it is', and gestured towards a rather grey council estate overlooking what I took to be Thurso Bay.

Thus it was, my co-traveller, my fellow vagrant, of some eight days, as lost as I was but far more carefree, left my van and my life hurling yet another empty can of McEwan's down the main street leading into Thurso as a gesture to the way the powers that be, have allowed Dounreay to pollute the countryside. I sat watching him walk down the alleyway to the estate, disappearing from view into a cluster of houses. I never saw him again.

I stopped a second or so to watch my companion leave and to take stock of my situation, now that my guide to those northern towns had taken leave of me. I reached on to the dashboard of the van, and took out a very tattered and 'seen better days' 1974 edition of the AA book one of my class had found (found – always a slightly dubious word where my class is concerned) and brought to school. I would, I decided after some slight deliberation, travel from Thurso to John O'Groats, take the A9 down the eastern coast to Inverness, travel to Perth, Glasgow, Carlisle and take the inevitable and totally predictable M6 southwards to home. I allowed myself a further three days of travelling, enjoying the occasional stay in a clean bed for a night or so, free from the emasculating sneer of my tinker companion. I reflected that without Jamie and his guided tour of undesirable places and equally undesirable people, my journey would be much quicker, though I had to admit far less interesting.

The van had decided to behave in a contrary manner once again, and as I turned the vehicle around in the main road, began to judder and belch clouds of black oily smoke, as if in disagreement of my retracing my steps to explore the tiny fishing village of Scrabster, a port once featured briefly in the ill-made, badly lit, Neil Gunn inspired film *The Silver Darlings* (a Scottish term for the once common, now far from common, herring).

An icy wind swept the harbour, as indeed the same icy wind is want to do summer and winter alike, ensuring that the harbour was deserted apart from one or two crabbers making none too concerted efforts at repairing rips in the netting of their creels, and a few patently obvious foreign tourists reading the notices concerning the departure and arrival of the ferry, the St Ola, at that time the only connecting sealink between Caithness and Orkney. The icy wind began to burrow through my threadbare 'wear anywhere' donkey coat weaving its way through my sweater and shirt, coming to rest in my bones, chilling their very marrow. I attempted a slightly less than half-hearted masculine smile, which degenerated into a shiver. Legend has it that the nephews of King Arthur, Gawain, Gareth and Gaheris were sons of Lot, King of the Orkney and the huge Celtic hound Cavall, a beast as large as a pony and as ferocious as a boar, was supposedly bred in the Orkneys where story has it, up until medieval times, the Orcadians regarded themselves as a race apart from the Scots.

As I stood shivering on the quayside wondering if it was wiser to brave the odours of my smelly van than stand in this vicious and cruel wind, an estate car pulled up carrying Barbour-jacketted passengers and a perch-like device known as a 'cadge', upon which were tied by leather thongs, known as jesses, two falcons, hooded and respectable and, at a safe distance, an unhooded wild-eyed male eyas goshawk. The driver too studied the poster advertising the times and departure of the ferry and returned to the car to his companions. They were obviously falconers (and austringers if one wishes to be accurate, for such is the term used for those with patience and calm enough to train a goshawk) on their way to Orkney to hawk grouse, though the presence of the goshawk, glaring as only goshawks can glare at the fellow occupants of the cadge, puzzled me as the grouse is a bird of considerable speed and certainly more than a match for a goshawk.

All aspects of grouse hunting, be it the rearing, shooting, hawking or even the obligatory hanging prior to the eating of the bird, are part of some curious and esoteric ritual. Grouse are not reared in the traditional manner of most game birds, hatched in incubators, reared under broody hens, turned loose in gradual stages, to make them progressively wilder and more wary of man, as are pheasants. Grouse are exclusively wild birds, indeed attempts to rear them in captivity have been largely unsuccessful. The glorious twelfth, a curious ritual indeed, when those who are well-heeled travel hundreds of miles and pay astronomic sums to shoot at and possibly hit, these partridge-sized birds, is preceded by months of predator control, but the success of the grouse shoot (depending, I suppose, on whether one is a grouse or a gunman) is determined to a large extent on the vagaries of the weather. A wet year – common on the moors of Scotland, and Orkney – drowns hundreds of chicks, if that is the correct name for young grouse, and likewise a dry year fails to provide the necessary food to rear them. The grouse shooting season too is often a short one for after the slaughter of the 12th the birds become too wily, too aware of the predatory nature of man to be suitable quarry for the gunman, and hence many grouse moors, even the more fashionable ones, become the hunting ground of falconers carrying the traditional enemies of the grouse, the peregrine, the saker, and even the rare and spectacular gyrfalcon, a large powerful peregrine-like bird, all of which have their mettle tried to the full by the speed and aerobatics of the most testing of quarry, the grouse.

However, if the grouse is a baffling and enigmatic creature so also is the falconer who pursues these birds. The better falconers are often as shy and wary of human company as the grouse themselves and reluctant to answer questions about their interests – questions much like as not are invariably ridiculous and inane for the sport is not one commonly encountered by the general public. The more inadequate of falconers is often more than ready to inform the public and relate often ridiculously exaggerated tales, usually dressing in embarrassingly archaic and flamboyant costumes to attract interest to their chosen hobby.

However, it was my unfortunate habit of staring at objects and people (staring in the animal kingdom is often the prelude to attack, in my case I'm afraid it often invites the selfsame attacks) that began to irritate the occupants of the estate car and finally caused them to enquire if anything was wrong or if I wanted something of them. As it was, all I could do was express interest in their wards but the fact that I knew something of falconry (I have kept and trained hawks) and knew something of the antiquated parlance which accompanies the sport, seemed to put them at ease and encourage them to talk about their falcons and their destination.

Ironically two of the hawks were peregrines, captive bred birds, (twenty years ago a captive bred peregrine made the world's newspapers but now they are not uncommon), but the Orkneys were the traditional home of the peregrines of the falconry-orientated Kings of Britain and Europe itself, and eyases, the peregrine chicks, were obtained by Orcadian boys swinging down the precipitous cliffs of the islands in rope baskets and taking the eyases just before they were ready to fly. The eyases were driven south, fed on the flesh of puppies, macabre as it may seem, until they reached the falconers of the south. Traditionally the peregrine, at least according to the much-quoted *Boke of St Albans*, was the bird of the baron or earl. Likewise the male or tiercel goshawk tethered at a safe distance from the falcons was the hawk of the poor man, too small to take a fully grown rabbit, but fast and plucky enough to show its mettle on most birds, other than the grouse of course.

The hawk of the poor man instinctively attracted me to it, clad as I was in my dirty donkey coat, travelling in my filthy Ford Escort and accompanied by two lurchers. Thus I suppose I was literally drawn to the bird and its owner. The hawk too was aviary bred, bred in fact not fifty miles away from my Lichfield home, and had cost its owner £286, slightly more than I was earning in a month. Seemingly my teacher's salary did not justify even the title of a poor man according to the list of the *Boke of St Albans*, for such a price would be well beyond me and my purse.

I ceased contemplating the birds and took stock of my own situation. What exactly did the Abbess, author of the book, mean by a 'poor man'? I had worked a lifetime in a profession, which not only did I despise, but whose members showed little more than derision for me. I had seldom missed a day, yet earned a pittance. Jamie who had left me in Thurso had probably seldom worked or contemplated a job, yet had all he desired, though God knows how he obtained his present wad of monies. My life, not the life of the typical member of society was out of kilter, trapezoid, not rectangular might best describe it. I had despised my father for his workshy habits, he was seldom employed and rarely could he keep a job, yet had it not been for my harridan mother he would have lived fairly happily, not prosperously but happily. On the other hand, I who had lived a bachelor life had been a work slave most of my life in a profession I hated. Somehow something was woefully wrong. I had achieved little by way of financial gain by my job, damnably little in fact, and not only had I obtained no job satisfaction, I had become dispirited, broken, lacking in self-confidence and aware only of my own supposed inadequacies. At that moment in time I realised that whatever happened I must quit my job and lead a life style I wanted regardless of the rules and regulations imposed by a quasi profession. Come what may I would get out of teaching, live the way I wished, suffer, if necessary, the financial privations which seem to accompany lack of employment but I would I vowed live the life I chose, not the life expected of me by the profession or the society whose children I simply child-minded rather than taught. Finally I did get the opportunity to get out but as usual I run ahead of my tale, beside which the manner of my departure from teaching is quite another story. I said goodbye to the falconers and strode back to my messy van, aware of my vow to leave teaching, the icy biting wind, and strangely a dull throbbing ache down my left arm.

POLLY

—11—

The Bottom has Fallen out of Pigs

'THE BOTTOM HAS fallen out of pigs, yet again,' announced Mr Loughrey, and though I found it hard not to snigger at the incongruous and painful double entendre, the sight of Mr Loughrey's pained face and his ham-like (a bad pun) arms made me desist. I had been 'driven in' again – how curious to be without Jamie to chide me for my lack of manhood and my willingness to pay for a night's sleep and a bath – on the A9 on the way to Inverness, and Mr Loughrey the owner of the said residence was also the owner of a large and seemingly unprofitable herd of large white pigs, out of which the bottom had apparently fallen. The said statement being nothing to do with the shaky disposition of a pig's derrière, but rather due to the fact that in the ever fluctuating world of pigs, there were decided bulls and bears in the market and this particular week pigs, live, snorting, pink and particoloured, were hitting an all time low, price-wise. I nodded my head in sympathy, for it is a sad thing to find that the bottom has fallen out of one's pigs.

I rather like pigs, I've taught several, and one or two of the four-footed variety as well. In point of fact about a year before my meeting with Mr Loughrey and his bottomless pigs, I'd acquired an American Duroc which I called Emma, a pretty beast my terriers had disliked on sight and Emma had inevitably fallen foul of my terrier bitch Pagan who had slashed, torn and just about killed the hapless piglet. Emma was four weeks old at the time, too young to wean, but I'd had her at this age to train as a retriever in the manner that Arkwright, the great eighteenth-century eccentric, had trained one and then audaciously and none too elegantly ridden her to hounds. Emma had been wrapped in blankets after her near fatal collision with Pagan, and Polly, my white German shepherd, had immediately come into milk and suckled the piglet. In next to no time Emma had become, to use psychological parlance 'imprinted' – she considered she was a dog, not a piglet, and within days she was trained to the standards expected by Arkwright. When introduced to other piglets she exploded into a state of terror, hid in the back of her pen and was terrified of the pair I'd bought to keep her company.

I made a considerable study of pigs simply because of Emma and no more interesting animal can be found, that's if you are not a Moslem or a Jew, for supposedly members of the said religious groups consider them to be haram, herem, or in simple English parlance, unclean. In point of fact pigs, given a chance, and they seldom are if the horrific Animal Rights posters are correct, are scrupulously clean and seldom, if ever, foul in their sleeping quarters. Why the pig and all things porcine are considered unclean was a little bewildering at least before my own pigs pushed over the flimsy fencing and strayed in the road. My bearded collie, as honest a worker as one could wish, went frantic trying to herd the swine back into the enclosure. They simply refused to be herded – and thereby lay the tale that pigs were unclean. The Koran and the Torah, the Moslem and the Jewish bibles, were written by nomads, people who wandered from place to place seeking pasture. Sheep, goats, even cattle, will respond to this sort of life but pigs, which refuse to be herded, are therefore suitable only for a more settled type of life. They did in fact symbolise a life, the settled life of the Canaanite, that the Jew and the Moslem despised. Thus the pig became regarded as unclean.

The northern races had no such qualms about pig meat. Take for instance the curious eating rituals associated with Christmas. Today we indulge in a two or three-day period of absolute gluttony, gobbling down an American bird, the turkey. It wasn't always so. Yule, the pagan festival of the closing of the year which was later to be replaced by the Christian Christmas, was an economic necessity rather than a ritualistic orgy of gluttony. At Yule when the grass was almost ungrazable, the geese were killed and eaten, and pigs were slaughtered and salted down. Almost every part of the pig can not only be eaten, but also preserved. Not so the vast quantities of blood which drain from the stricken pigs which were and are traditionally killed by cutting their throats, and rather barbarically I've always thought, bleeding them to death. The Vikings and other Nordic peoples were loathe to waste this blood and hence the traditional Nordic Christmas feast consisted of blood sausage, blood and fat preserved and flavoured with bitter herbs and seaweed in the membranous small intestines of sheep or pigs.

Pigs were therefore popular with the Northern Aryans. They were a little more of a problem to the Egyptians. Early Egyptians valued the pig which not only ploughed up the land, cleared woods and thickets, but also allowed the earliest settler to plant grain in the tiny hoof marks left by the pig. Then quite suddenly the pig became a little less of a farmer's friend. In a matter of a hundred years the pig fell out of favour and became a creature to be despised. Perhaps one of the priests or ruling potentates became allergic to pork, and lesser people fashionably followed suit. Perhaps nomadic people like the Hyksos took over control of their land and brought the traditional nomadic anti-porcine taboos with them. Tacitus, a Roman historian, believed that pig flesh caused leprosy – uncooked it can certainly introduce tapeworms into the human body – but leprosy? Well, that's going a bit far perhaps.

Pigs were perhaps brought to Britain aboard small Celtic ships, but the chances are that the original dwellers simply domesticated the wild boar stealing its very young piglets, and this in itself would be an act more worthy of a George Medal than a rapping from the preservationists. The wild boar is just about the gamest beast imaginable and the ancients were quick to realise this. The once popular and now lampooned name Everhard means brave as a boar, and the fight put up by a surly old male or a sow protecting her young is bloody and ferocious beyond belief. Boars such as the one which appeared in Calydon (a popular spot in Greek legends) became ferocious dragon-type adversaries which tempted the worthies of the province to test their manhood by tracking the boars down and killing them. Shakespeare could not have seen one, they were nearly extinct by his day, but their reputation lived on, and Shapespeare wrote of them, 'Where they strike their crooked tushes slay', either by deep wounds, disembowelment, or simply as a result of gangrene introduced by the goring, for the tusks of pigs are hardly the cleanest of weapons. Traditionally the killing of a boar amounted to almost a battle. Until the invention of gunpowder the rind-like skin could hardly be penetrated by arrows other than the needle-type bodkins and the hunt for a difficult and destructive boar coming into the 'lists' at above 300 lbs began with cornering a boar using dogs, while the knight in his padded armour, fired a barrage of arrows into it. Meanwhile, various hunters with spears fitted with a crossbar to prevent the impaled boar racing down the shaft and despatching the hunters, jabbed and stabbed the cornered and furious-natured boar, allowing a knight to come up and slay the animal with a sword. Traditional pigsticking occurred only in India – a pastime of the Raj princes who also tested their manhood on the wild boar, an Indian species just as game and eager to fight as the European variety.

The English domesticated pig was little more than a tamed wild boar with perhaps a slight dash of even more primitive blood added, and as late as 1700 pigs were still born striped and bristly as were their wild ancestors. They were also dangerous not only to their owners, but to innocent bystanders, almost by custom, the traditional victims of all the most savage attacks of animals. Pigs were allowed to wander the towns at one time probably doing a good job eating waste, filth and cadavers of cats, dogs and other less savoury messes dumped by the far from hygienic British. Pigs were outlawed in most towns not so much for the mess they caused – the streets were a quagmire anyway, but because they presented a hazard to life and limb of anyone who intentionally or inadvertently upset them. As late as 1760 an Irish pig, a long, lean, leggy, tassel-throated version of the English swine, killed and ate a child (and was publicly executed for the crime).

So how on earth did the savage, near-wild, razor-backed British pig develop into the fat-jowled grunting porker of today, pink-skinned and a suitable character for a children's story book, even though the bottoms seem to be falling out of the said animals? Well, in the 1700s massive improvements took place in British agriculture and huge sheep replaced the minute, scraggy Soay types which produced a carcase only slightly bigger than a hare. Travellers from China brought back fat white pigs which their oriental breeders who lived in a land-hungry country, had prevented from wandering free. They were kept in styes, paddocks and even cages aboard junk-type houseboats. These pigs fed on a protein-rich diet fattened quickly. They were mated with our own swine and eureka, the striped piglet was replaced by the sort of fat cuddly swine of the type who built straw houses and fell prey to smooth-talking wolves. The old English breeds – well, they simply went out of fashion – they foraged well, lived on beech mast, acorns and waste, but they fattened slowly.

The British are a curious race and only after the extinction of a breed do they seem interested in preserving the said breed. In the 1960s the Iron Age settlement at Butser Hill was excavated and a museum-type settlement with primitive Iron Age animals was set up there. Well, there were Soay sheep identical to their Iron Age counterparts readily available, practically unsaleable perhaps, but readily available nevertheless, and some parks still sported the white primitive cattle kept by the Celts, but the Iron Age pig, the razor-backed striped swine, a stone's throw from the wild and ferocious boar – had gone the way of all flesh, an apt choice of phrase if ever there was one. Henson of the Rare Breeds Trust came to the rescue. He mated, with some difficulty one should add, the red Tamworth – a fairly primitive pig and so nearly extinct in Britain that Henson had to import them from New Zealand – with wild boars. The first crosses were truculent, difficult to manage and hardly of the type which a curious group of totally unsuitable people who hoped to live out a year of Iron Age spartan-type life, would willingly keep. Henson experimented further and came up with a near replica of the beast kept by pre-Roman Celtic tribesmen. The Iron Age settlers were made the subject of a TV documentary, but failed at their Iron Age lifestyle. They were not the type of alternative livers I'd have chosen for such a soul-destroying year, anyway. Henson was far more successful. His end product can be seen at Butser Hill and at his Rare Breeds Trust in Stowe. Commercially – well, in this age of intensive farming so much disliked by the Animal Rights group – Henson was perhaps not successful. To the alternative livers, a group who want to turn the agricultural clock back four or five centuries, then perhaps a pig which will live on waste cabbage, leaves, bread scraps and with a suitable place to forage, would have been successful. The new type was bred simply to be an ornament to a Celtic-type village, a test of Henson's incredible ingenuity, but the alternative living groups are quick to point out that the proteinous animal feed supplies, the meat and bone-meal supplements, the vast piles of small undersized, unsuitable fish are giving out, and the sea has been milked dry and now needs to rest up a while and the vegetable protein supplies, the soya, the horse bean *etc*, should be used to feed the Third World, not cramped, crotchety, dispirited pigs and slatted board-fed, veal-producing calves. Perhaps there is room for the scavenging pigs, slow to grow but economical to rear, but it seems unlikely. The trend seems to be towards a vegetarian, or a lacto-vegetarian homo sapiens. Coronaries, and cancer of the bowel are attributed, rightly or wrongly, to the intake of animal protein, so perhaps even the scavenging pig of early Medieval times would be as out of place as his more fastidious sty-fed counterpart out of which the bottom has fallen.

China, now there's a country that takes its pigs seriously, though in the light of what is to follow perhaps seriously is scarcely the word. Just as sheep, cattle and goats seem to be tailor-made for a nomadic agricultural system, so the pig slots in to the way of life of the settled farmer, particularly the settled farmer of crowded China. China once boasted a huge number of varieties of pigs ranging from large European-type creatures, scarcely more than domesticated wild boars to tiny pot-bellied pigs which were so bloated they could scarcely walk. In point of fact, the rotund abdomen was functional for it contained a huge length of gut which allowed the pig to digest poor grade herbage and exist if not thrive on it – the Vietnamese pot-bellied pig is still able to do this. The pig in fact entered the Chinese way of life and when one of the early Chin emperors decided to lampoon the natives of certain provinces, he chose, a little like Jesus perhaps, to use parables to bring about ridicule and what better animal to include in his parables than the good old-fashioned Chinese pig. Unlike Jesus, however, his parables are near the knuckle. I'll explain.

Canton, a province of China, was once notorious for the slothful nature of its people. Cantonese meant simply idle in fact. The story goes, a monk was once wandering through Canton when he espied a slovenly man seated on a mound of garbage, fanning himself with an almost leafless branch. Around him reigned filth, confusion, and an unwholesome air of neglect and decay. 'Priest,' shouted the reclining sluggard, 'be so good as to catch up my young pig,' and the priest dutifully caught up the piglet, as I suppose helpful priests are wont to do. 'Would you be so good as to castrate the piglet?' asked the still reclining peasant, and the now rather alarmed priest, after he was persuaded the act of emasculation would not damage either his soul nor the immortal spirit of the pig, did so. 'Now', continued the sluggard, 'would you stitch its scrotum to ensure that sepsis does not harm the beast, and while he is still in your arms would you ring its nose to prevent it damaging the rice crop by its rooting?' The priest frowned at the idleness of the peasant, but nonetheless did so. 'Also,' went on the peasant to the now very angry priest, 'would you tether the piglet to the stake to prevent its escape?' 'Look,' exploded the priest, his Buddhist composure now well and truly ruffled, 'why don't you marry and perhaps your children will do these tasks for you?' 'What an excellent idea,' beamed the peasant. 'Priest, on your travels have you encountered any pregnant women?'

Likewise, the provinces of South China had an apparently well justified reputation for being miserly, and such biting avarice was responsible for producing the following parable yet once again using the pig as an unfortunate fulcrum for the joke. A South Chinese peasant is boasting about the virtues of his pig. 'No one has ever had such a pig,' he boasts to his neighbour. 'No one. Last month my son was drowning in the lake and my pig raced in and rescued him. My wife was attacked by savage dogs – the pig drove them off. A burglar broke into my house – the pig attacked him. Such a pig,' he repeated proudly. The neighbour is impressed but questions, 'Why does the pig have a wooden leg?' 'Do you expect me to eat an animal of such value in one sitting?' replied the farmer angrily!

Last, but certainly not least, was the problem which was occurring near the borders of Manchuria, where the peasants, one step ahead of the hostile nomads of the steppes, lived a hard and tough life, and were the brunt of most Chinese jokes, for the Chinese hid their fear of these often very barbarous people by ridiculing their lack of education – few of the peasants of these provinces wrote or even spoke traditional Chinese – and accusing them of a variety of malpractices, ranging from cannibalism to sexual perversion – cue for tale. A haughty Chinese tax inspector is visiting a farm along the Manchurian frontier south of the

Marco Polo bridge and assessing the value of the goods of the loutish peasant farming the land. 'Peasant,' the inspector says rather snootily, 'the weight of this pig, if you please.' To the amazement of the tax inspector, the peasant suddenly grabs the pig, bites its penis, and with the pig suspended from his mouth, he utters, twixt clenched teeth, '168 lb.' The tax inspector has recovered his composure by this time and disparagingly chides the peasant on his highly peculiar behaviour, insisting that the peasant weighs the pig on the Imperial scales. The scales register 168 lb exactly and the inspector is just recovering from his astonishment when the peasant gleefully volunteers, 'All the family have the gift.' As quick as a flash his young son upends a diminutive piglet in the selfsame manner and announces, '12 lb 6 oz.' The scales agree exactly with the son's assessment. 'Go fetch your mother,' shouts the peasant, now ecstatic about the bewilderment displayed by the collector, 'Go fetch your mother,' and the boy also delighted races home, but returns to say, 'Mother will be some little time, she is weighing the other tax collector.' So much for China and its ever present pigs, and thank God the beast hasn't had such an impact on our British way of life – or has it?

Funnily enough it has, and while we haven't had a spate of savants eager and willing to incorporate things porcine into our way of life, the pig has so to speak entered into the English language in a big way. Like the cat, the pig features in a variety of common sayings, and one such saying incorporates both the cat and the pig. 'Pig in a poke', buying an object or animal unseen is derived from the malpractice of Medieval fairground shysters and rogues who offered a 'piglet' in a sack to the unsuspecting sucker. The piglet was in fact a fat cat. The sucker having bought his 'pig in the poke' took his buy home only to 'let the cat out of the bag'.

Piggyback has nothing to do with riding a pig in this manner, though Jane, Duchess of Gordon, who in 1770 took a bet that she would ride a pig down the High Street of Edinburgh and, undignified as it may appear, did ride a bucking, biting boar and won her wager. No, the saying has nothing to do with pigs, but is a corruption of the Italian word 'pigga' meaning a child, hence piggaback is the manner in which Italian ladies carried their children, not their pigs.

Pig iron – a term reminiscent and evocative of Coalbrookdale, the air of that Shropshire village sulphurous and choking, the skyline a dull red at night, has quite a lot to do with pigs. The iron was run into a great mould resembling a sow and small ingots of iron running off the main body of the iron were said to resemble piglets. I worked in such a foundry once, a hellish place, dark and satanic, and frightening as only places which produce white hot products can be. I stayed six months, long enough to learn the grim humour of the workers, whose sensitivity had long since been sweated out by the searing heat of the furnaces. A man had apparently fallen into the vats the day I arrived – a horrendous death, the sort of ending more suited to a nightmare than to reality – and one of the older smelters had lamented that the bone content of the poor wretch had ruined the iron of that particular melt. Sick humour – well, perhaps not, maybe simply a way of mentally shutting off the awesome danger with which the workers lived on a matter-of-fact, day-to-day basis.

'What happened to the man who invented all the dirty jokes?' Mr Loughrey jerked me out of my dreams of pigs and pig-orientated language with a lament that he had heard nothing sexually funny to cheer him up for weeks. I was about to regale him with the three Chinese tales but on consideration, glancing at his dismal Landrace pig jowls and sad expression, I decided against it. Nothing remotely porcine would have been suitable to cheer up a depressed pig breeder who had had the bottom fall out of his wards. I thought better of telling him the three off-centre Chinese jokes, paid my £6.00 bed and breakfast fee and clanged southwards towards Inverness.

POT PLANT

—12—

Assassins and Drop Outs

'HOW FAR ARE you wanting to go?' I had stopped to pick up an anoraked hitch-hiker who stood, soaked to the skin, haversack packed to the rim, on the edge of the A9 just south of Golspie. 'Oh God,' I groaned aloud, as the boy who answered 'Birmingham' to my question, folded himself into the dirty van and displayed a host of badges, all a bit anti-social, some slightly rude and two which proclaimed to the world his desire to 'Make pot legal'. I nodded. He slammed the door, and I prepared myself for three hundred and eighty miles of hand-jiving, with-it-man, died-out-in-the-1960s repartee which was destined to bore me silly. I'm not exactly against drug abuse, I believe everyone has a right to do pretty well what he or she wishes providing, and this is a very big providing, I'm afraid, it doesn't hurt or inconvenience others, and me in particular. I'd taught a variey of lunatics who took chemically propelled trips to brighter than bright lands using season tickets ranging from Evo Stick to cocaine, and I've never interfered in their way of life. I've even identified a few in rather dark and fortunately very cold mortuaries, unfortunates who found it a little late to mend their ways. What does get up my nose, no, not cocaine, is the perpetual teenybopper, 16–55 years old, who is not content to dope himself in peace and travel silently to his multi-coloured, soporific wonderland, but must boast of his fascination for narcotics, ram his interests down each and every person's throat and wear regalias to state to all the world that the said person is like as not to be 'under the influence', particularly at the time of his arrest. I've given dozens of lifts to such people and far from finding them interesting, they seem, to the last one, to be anachronisms, type-cast for a 1960s we've-just-started-the-permissive-society film, whose every other word is hash or pot and all police are called pigs. I steeled myself for ten hours of boredom, and hoped that my ability to shut off from pointless conversations would serve me in good stead. As it was we had scarcely reached Inverness when the conversation had turned to why pot harmed no one. I didn't rise to the bait and ask the customary and well-expected, 'Why do you do it? What do you get out of it?' thereby evoking a spate of righteous indignation which makes Tom Paine's *Rights of Man* seem as logical as Dr Seuss's *Cat in the Hat* monologue. As I said I've given dozens of pathetic characters like this lifts, and I've learned not to respond to the well-rehearsed question and answer routine with which people of this ilk seem all too familiar, and for the want of a better word, thrive. I turned down the shutters of my mind and tried my best to switch off mentally as we refuelled in Inverness and set out on the rabbit-strewn road over the Grampians and the Cairngorms to Perth.

My own age group copped for the away-from-it-all, dropping-out-of-the-rat-race era, but somehow just missed the 'with it' drugs scene epoch. I've never smoked, not even conventional stuff, though when I realised that my sweet bird of youth was not only on the wing but likely to be a geriatric dodo, I did hit the bottle for about six months. In fact my total knowledge of what today is called the drugs scene (a left over from the 1960s if I ever heard one) is Eric Ambler and an interest in blacker than black secret societies and even if I haven't whetted the reader's interest by these comments I shall nevertheless explain.

Ambler is one of the best detective thriller writers this century has produced. True, he is not into the birds, booze and brutality Mike Hammer type of book, ten bottles of bourbon, ten birds a day, but Ambler not only researches his characters well, but does a fair job on historical data and forensic science. I had been introduced to him, not in the flesh, more's the pity, by a train journey when, having nothing to do, and not having the foresight to buy something to read, I'd found a copy of his book *Mask Of Dimetrios*, and later watched Sidney Greenstreet overact through the film of the same name. Dimetrios is not only a drug smuggler, he is, according to Ambler, a drug user, specialising in opium, heroin and morphine. (Whatever happened to opium and it was so fashionable at one time, now not even 'way out' people use it.)

In point of fact there isn't a heck of a lot of difference between opium and heroin, chemically speaking, or from the point of view of its effects either. The users of both not only seem to die with alarming regularity, but for some reason the Chinese seem to be able to take both and also kick the habit whenever they wish. Opium is made from poppies, not the good old-fashioned, hairy-leaved red field poppy of the sort found in cornfields and on the lapels of Remembrance Day donators, but a sort of blue-green smooth-leaved poppy with white or purple flowers called peony or carnation flowering poppies by gardeners who can't seem to control the riotous seeding habits of the plant which seems to pop up in every hedgerow from you know where to John O'Groats. The Far East and Turkey grows millions of acres of these poppies, but there isn't a damned thing that anyone can do about it – the seeds are crushed for cooking oil and thus the plant has its legitimate uses. When the flowers fall, however, opium gatherers above the age of twelve – for those under the age of twelve are liable to be small, and hence must work in the opium-filled vapour layer amidst the foliage of the plant, and by inhaling the vapour become addicted to opium long before adulthood – swarm over the field and neatly slice into the seed heads of the poppy. A white latex sap appears from the cut and this is left to harden. If the sap is old, codeine – a common non-addictive pain killer – is extracted from it. If it is fresh it is called opium and in this form it was once smoked in Opium Dens and sold as a pain killer throughout Europe. De Quincy, a poor pathetic Lake District poet, earned scarcely more than a few pounds from baring his heart about his sad little habits in *Confessions of an Opium Eater*. Derivatives of opium were used as pain killers for operations particularly at sea, for sea-going surgeons for some reason or other sat less taxing examinations than did those whose incompetence killed people on land. Men whose legs were all but torn off by gunshot wounds, received amputations by being dosed with laudanum (an opium derivative), leg sawn off as quickly as possible and the stump plunged into molten tar to caulk, cauterise and give an antiseptic dressing to the wound – an act to make anyone's eyes water, believe me. Likewise another drug, morphine, made by adding vinegar and hydrochloric acid to an opium base was sold over the counter particularly after typhus and cholera induced such a state of dysentery that little apart from morphine could ease the fury of the illness. Heroin – one step further was used to relieve pain in patients with terminal illnesses – and is still used for such. So the poppy and its derivatives are extremely useful, and it is only the crazier element and their misuse of opiates that have brought the drugs to discredit.

'Yeh, it isn't so much the hard drugs we want to legalise,' the loon was still pontificating on the merits of chemically propelled trips to unreal lands. (I looked up and realised we'd reached Perth.) 'All we want is to have pot made legal – it's less addictive than nicotine. Who ever heard of pot causing any harm?' Who indeed, mate, who indeed, but there are many who would disagree with your theory that the drug causes no ill effects.

Pot or hashish is a derivative of Indian hemp, a plant similar in size and effect to the herb which would grow if ordinary fishermen's hemp seed was allowed to germinate – which it isn't as it's treated with heat to make sure that the fish don't go around looking pie-eyed. A handful of bird seed thrown on someone's compost heap, however, will usually produce a few rather tall plants which may not bring the butterflies but will certainly attract the narcotics squad. Tale has it that one of the largest hashish hauls in the Midlands was made after some old lady had mentioned to her friendly neighbourhood police officer that there were enormous plants sprouting out of the corner of her garden where she had flung her cage bird droppings. A fortune in cannabis was quietly reaped by the drugs squad and quietly disposed of, but as regards to the drug doing no one any harm – well perhaps that is another tale.

During the closing days of the turbulent and rather crazy eleventh century, three youths at school in the Middle East took a heroic and rather juvenile blood oath that whosoever made it up the steep and precipitous slope to fame would help the others. The three boys, a dreamy-eyed tent-maker's son and poet called Omar Khayyam, a rather earnest young man called Nizam Al Mulk, and a strange sinister aesthetic boy called Hassan Sabah, swore their Biggles-type vows, and straight away forgot about them. Later Al Mulk became grand vizier to the Seljuk rulers of Iran and began to remember the schoolboy oath. Out of good nature, or perhaps a sense of honour, he sought out the other two, only to find that Omar had renounced the world and its splendour and wanted only a glass dome under which he could watch the stars. Hasan Sabah, however, had disappeared into the mystic quarter of Cairo where he mingled with a set of bona fide magicians called the Fidawi who were teaching what can only be described as a form of death cult. The youth absorbed these teachings with frightening enthusiasm and years later emerged to take the impregnable fortress of Alamut or the Eagles Nest in Khorosan, Iraq, with a technique more akin to a missionary rather than a conqueror. Once installed he founded one of the most peculiar and terrifying societies ever. Sabah realised that the most susceptible and gullible peasants could be transformed into the most devoted acolytes if given some form of traumatic experience. Sabah, therefore, brought about one of the most incredible sleights of hand imaginable. Muslims are not allowed to drink alcohol, hence a glass of wine laced with marajuana or hashish had a devastating effect and laid the poor gullible peasants out cold. The peasant awoke in a magic garden where the most beautiful women catered for his every desire and fountains gushed wine. Three days later one of these enchantresses brought the now thoroughly bewildered future convert yet another glass of hashish-laced wine. The wretched, and now probably not only confused but demented chap, now woke up back in Hassan Sabah's apartment deranged, disorientated but willing to believe literally anything Sabah would tell him. Sabah now informed the victim that he had been to Paradise and given a taste of its pleasures and with the aplomb of a hyped-up double glazing salesman explained that with a few more easy payments, Paradise for all eternity could be his. Once the sucker had taken the bait, and those who didn't probably didn't live long enough to leave the apartment, Sabah began a rigorous seven-year training course after which all that was left of the poor devil's mind was now really confused and even more bewildered. Sabah, who had now adopted a god-like power, was obeyed implicitly and the wretch was armed with a dagger and sent forth to murder anyone who had incurred his master's displeasure. Nizam Al Mulk, the genial childhood friend of Hassan Sabah, was the first to bite the dust probably to show that the master needed no one, and literally no one seemed safe from these fanatics. Christians at prayer in church arose to find a wild-eyed lunatic driving a dagger into their hearts, and Arab diplomats surrounded by trusted guards were horrified to find their most faithful followers whip off their turbans revealing the skull cap of the order and plunge a knife upwards into their chests. A reign of terror gripped the Middle East while Turk and Crusader lived uneasy lives fearful of assassination. The band became known in fact as the Hashishyun, or eaters of hashish, and this in time was corrupted to assassin. The ending of the tale, for all good tales need an ending – well, the Assassins, who continued long after the death of Al Sabah, overplayed their hands somewhat. A new power had arisen in Asia, a band of adventurers called the Mongols had crushed everything in their path on their way from the Steppes to Egypt and foolishly the Assassins fell foul of them. By a monumental error of judgement by the Grand Master of the Assassins, Jingi the grandson of the Mongol leader was murdered, and the Mongols crushed the fanatical band like grapes. As you say, my friend, hashish (pot) does no one any harm.

We travelled south bypassing Glasgow and arrived in Carlisle where I ate and the youth disappeared into the toilet to emerge glassy-eyed but sadly more eloquent than ever, though talkative is a more apt word than eloquent. He had become a bore, a self-opinionated buffoon who believed that drugs and drugs alone were efficacious in solving the problems of a troubled world. His effect on me was profound for now I cannot, try as I might, feel anything other than disgust for those whose only thrill in life is achieved by the make-believe world of narcotics. I would, and still will, defend with vigour the rights of anyone to take whatever poison or soporific he may, but three hundred and fifty miles of boredom of non-stop twaddle about the merits of narcotics is more than flesh, blood and DBP can stand.

By Carlisle I was regretful that Jamie had left me and I felt a nostalgic longing for his overripe body odour, his sharp cutting inconsistency, and total intolerance to anything he could not understand. Jamie at least was interesting in a peculiar sort of way, as was every character, outlandish or pathetic, that I had met on my ten-day trip north, but now I was trapped, trapped in the presence of that most uninteresting of creatures, the supercilious bore, the Peter Pan who refuses to grow up and face reality preferring to plummet, wallow and dwell in his opiate/hashish-flavoured wonderland. My week and a half of escapism had allowed me to meet a variety of real people, people with problems, people content with their lot in life. I took a silent vow to somehow vet all hitch-hikers before giving them lifts – making sure all 'Make pot legal' badge bearing bores would be barred from travelling with me.

I had endured three hundred and fifty soul-destroying miles of trying to make conversation with a man who knew only glib comments like 'Make pot legal' and similar claptrap.

He left my company at Burton-on-Trent.

'Have you ever seen anyone really high, really high, on hash?' he asked, lapsing into his Mid-Atlantic accent.

I nodded, bored out of my mind by his incessant chunter about his obsession.

'Yes,' I muttered, 'he threw himself on the floor – and missed.' I slammed the door of the van and drove towards Lichfield and home.

BEER CAN

Epilogue

I ARRIVED IN Lichfield just before noon on Saturday. It was a flag day, but it's always a flag day in Lichfield, each and every Saturday. Bored middle-class housewives literally come to life in Lichfield every Saturday, standing in strategic spots jangling tins and smiling inanely. Any event seemingly merits a flag day in Lichfield, and during my stay there I have been ambushed, and brow-beaten into donating sums to charities ranging from senile lighthouse men to unmarried Peruvian prisoners; political prisoners of course. In fact any red-blooded man would do anything to escape the tin-jangling large-toothed smiling females who leap out from behind corners in Lichfield. I drove through, watching sickened donators take circuitous routes to avoid the collectors only to bump into more seemingly identical females and finally succumb to buying flags.

I turned down the lane to my cottage and pulled up outside my rambling ill-built home, the van throwing out clouds of black, you're-lucky-to-have-made-it-home smoke. Ian, suspecting dog thieves who are invariably as disreputable looking as I am, raced out and uttered a sigh of relief on seeing me.

'You look tired . . . sir,' he added 'sir' as an afterthought. (A teacher is, so those who know believe, certainly on the way out when 'sir' comes as an afterthought.) 'And ill . . . sir' – yet another afterthought.

'It's just some pains in my chest and down my arms, Ian,' I said wearily. 'They'll vanish after I rest up a day or so,' I added, confidently unaware of the problems such pains were to bring.

I sat in the van and reflected on my life as Ian almost automatically took out the dogs to kennel them, and systematically began to unpack my soiled and evil-smelling luggage. I had left in a welter of depression, only to return even more depressed and thoroughly discontent with my lot in life. The kaleidoscope of people I had met on my travels had convinced me not only that the dolce vita was hard to find, but that I was not only ill-fitted to a vagrant life, but also socially inadequate. My life's work to date had amounted to a hastily scribbled book without much content and with even less depth of meaning – not a lot to show for forty years of unhappiness. I began to wallow in self-pity, but Ian snapped me out of my thoughts with the gaucherie only a fourteen-year-old is allowed to manifest.

'Didn't know you was an . . . an . . . .' He made about four attempts at the word 'alcoholic' before finally getting it right. My raised eyebrows and quizzical expression made him elaborate. 'Look . . . sir,' (another afterthought).

He reached down behind the passenger seat, and like a conjurer pulling rabbits from a hat produced a full can of McEwan's Bitter. I stared at the can which Ian shook vigorously to convince himself of its contents. I remembered its owner, legal or otherwise, and reflected on the characters I had met on the road.

'There's a lot you don't know, Ian,' I spat out dramatically. 'Come to think of it, there's a lot I don't know.'